Stories, Songs, and Poetry to Teach Reading and Writing

Literacy through Language

Robert A. McCracken and
Marlene J. McCracken

American Library Association   Chicago and London 1986

Designed by Ellen Pettengell

Drawings by Diane Colquhoun

Cover design by Natalie Wargin

Composed by Ampersand Inc.
in Itek Palatino on a Digitek
typesetting system

Printed on 50-pound Glatfelter,
a pH-neutral stock, and
bound in 10-point Carolina
cover stock by
Edwards Brothers, Inc.
∞

This publication is also available
from the Teachers College Press
of Columbia University,
1234 Amsterdam Avenue,
New York, New York 10027.

Library of Congress Cataloging-in-Publication Data

McCracken, Robert A.
    Stories, songs, and poetry to teach reading and
writing.

    Bibliography: p.
    1. Language arts (Elementary) 2. Children—Language.
I. McCracken, Marlene J. II. Title.
LB1576.M185   1986   372.6′044   86-1150
ISBN 0-8389-0450-5

Contents

Acknowledgments v

Introduction ix

1 Literacy as Natural Learning 1

2 Reading Readiness—Extending the Lap 12

3 Reading as Apprehension and Prediction 22

4 Beginning Reading from the Pocket Chart 34

5 Spelling 62

6 Beginning Writing 73

7 Poetry and Song 102

8 Paragraph Writing 121

9 Research 135

10 For Parents and Nonteachers 141

Bibliography 153

Acknowledgments

Excerpt from *Time Cat* by Lloyd Alexander. Copyright © 1963 by Holt, Rinehart & Winston, 1963.

Excerpt from *At Mary Bloom's* written and illustrated by Aliki. Copyright © 1976 by Greenwillow Books.

Excerpt from *Who Sank the Boat?* by Pamela Allen. Copyright © 1982 by Pamela Allen. Reprinted by permission of Coward-McCann, Inc., Hamish Hamilton Limited, and Thomas Nelson Australia.

Excerpt from pp. 111–12 in *Devil's Donkey* by Bill Brittain; pictures by Andrew Glass. Text copyright © 1981 by William Brittain. Reprinted by permission of Harper & Row, Publishers, Inc.

"Bugs" from *The Fish with the Deep Sea Smile* by Margaret Wise Brown. Copyright © 1938 by E. P. Dutton; renewed 1965 by Roberta B. Rauch. Reprinted by permission of Roberta B. Rauch.

"The Rabbit Skip" from *Nibble, Nibble: Poems for Children* by Margaret Wise Brown (Addison-Wesley), A Young Scott Book. Text copyright © 1959 by William R. Scott, Inc. Reprinted by permission of Harper & Row, Publishers, Inc.

Excerpt from *Where Have You Been?* by Margaret Wise Brown. Hastings House, Publishers, New York, 1952; new enlarged edition, 1981.

Excerpts from *The Sword in the Tree* by Clyde Robert Bulla; illustrated by Paul Galdone (Thomas Y. Crowell Co.). Copyright © 1956 by Clyde Robert Bulla. Reprinted by permission of Harper & Row, Publishers, Inc.

Excerpt from pp. 71–72 of *Good-bye, Chicken Little* by Betsy Byars. Copyright © 1979 by Betsy Byars. Reprinted by permission of Harper & Row, Publishers, Inc.

Excerpts from pages 8–9, 18, 42, 45 in *The Sense of Wonder* by Rachel Carson. Text copyright © 1956 by Rachel L. Carson. Reprinted by permission of Harper & Row, Publishers, Inc.

Excerpt from *The Chocolate Touch* by Patrick Keene Catling. Copyright © 1979 by William Morrow & Co.

Excerpt from *Going for a Walk* by Beatrice Schenk de Regniers. Copyright © 1961 by Beatrice Schenk de Regniers. Reprinted by permission of Harper & Row, Publishers, Inc.

Excerpt from *The Three Little Pigs* by Paul Galdone. Copyright © 1970 by Paul Galdone. Reprinted by permission of Clarion Books, a Houghton Mifflin Company, and William Heinemann Ltd.

Excerpt from *Where's Spot?* by Eric Hill. Copyright © 1980 by Eric Hill. Reprinted by permission of G. P. Putnam's Sons and William Heinemann Ltd.

Excerpt from *A House Is a House for Me* by Mary Ann Hoberman. Copyright © Mary Ann Hoberman, 1978. Reprinted by permission of Viking Penguin, Inc.

Excerpt from *Rain* by Robert Kalan. Copyright © 1978 by Greenwillow Books.

Excerpt from *John Henry, an American Legend* by Ezra Jack Keats (Pantheon, 1965). Reprinted by permission of the Ezra Jack Keats Foundation.

"Think of It" by Bette Killion from *Poetry Place Anthology*. Copyright © 1983 by The Instructor Publications Inc.

Excerpt from *Blackie and Marie* by Marta Koci. Copyright © 1981 by William Morrow & Co.

Excerpt from *Good Night Little One* by Robert Kraus. Text copyright © 1973 by Robert Kraus. Reprinted by permission of Windmill Books, a division of Simon & Schuster, Inc.

Excerpt from *Whose Mouse Are You?* by Robert Kraus. Text copyright © 1970 by Robert Kraus. Reprinted by permission of Macmillan Publishing Company.

"Bugs" in *Dogs & Dragons, Trees & Dreams*: A Collection of Poems by Karla Kuskin. Copyright © 1962 by Karla Kuskin. Reprinted by permission of Harper & Row, Publishers, Inc.

First stanza of "If I Were a . . . " from *Dogs & Dragons, Trees & Dreams*: A Collection of Poems by Karla Kuskin. Copyright © 1964 by Karla Kuskin. Reprinted by permission of Harper & Row, Publishers, Inc.

Excerpt from *Brown Bear, Brown Bear, What Do You See?* A Kin/Der Owl Book, by Bill Martin, Jr. Copyright © 1971 by Holt, Rinehart & Winston, Publishers. Used by permission of the publisher. All rights reserved.

"Why I Did Not Reign" from *It Doesn't Always Have to Rhyme* by Eve Merriam. Copyright © 1964 by Eve Merriam. All rights reserved. Reprinted by permission of Marian Reiner for the author.

Excerpt from *When We Were Very Young* by A. A. Milne. Copyright © 1924 by E. P. Dutton, renewed 1952 by A. A. Milne. Reprinted by permission of the publisher, E. P. Dutton, a division of New American Library.

Excerpt from pages 111–12 in *Sibir, My Discovery of Siberia* by Farley Mowat (McClelland & Stewart, 1973). Reprinted by permission of Farley Mowat.

Excerpt from pp. 1–2 "The Little Old Woman and Her Pig" from *The Little Old Woman and Her Pig, and Ten Other Stories* by Anne Rockwell (Thomas Y. Crowell Co.). Copyright © 1979 by Anne Rockwell. Reprinted by permission of Harper & Row Publishers, Inc., and Curtis Brown, Ltd., London.

Excerpt from *Bambi* by Felix Salten, translated by Whittaker Chambers and published by Simon & Schuster, a division of Gulf & Western, 1956. Reprinted by permission of the Executor of the Felix Salten Estate, the translator, and Jonathan Cape Ltd.

Excerpt from *Seven Little Monsters*, written and illustrated by Maurice Sendak. Copyright © 1975 by Diogenes Verlag AG Zurich. Copyright © 1977 by

Maurice Sendak. Reprinted by permission of Harper & Row, Publishers, Inc., New York, and The Bodley Head, London.

Excerpt from *Dance Away* by George Shannon. Copyright © 1982 by Greenwillow Books.

Excerpt from *Lizard's Song* by George Shannon. Copyright © 1981 by Greenwillow Books.

Excerpt from *The Piney Woods Peddler* by George Shannon. Copyright © 1981 by Greenwillow Books.

Excerpt from *Is Anyone Here?* by Mina Lewiton Simon. Text copyright © 1967 Mina Lewiton Simon. Reprinted with permission of Atheneum Publishers.

Excerpt from *1 Is One* by Tasha Tudor (Rand McNally, 1956). Reprinted by permission of Tasha Tudor.

Excerpt from *The Judge* by Harve and Margot Zemach. Copyright © 1969 by Harve and Margot Zemach. Reprinted by permission of Farrar, Straus, and Giroux, Inc.

Introduction

I remembered one morning when I discovered a cocoon in the bark of a tree, just as a butterfly was making a hole in its case and preparing to come out. I waited a while, but it was too long appearing and I was impatient. I bent over it and breathed on it to warm it. I warmed it as quickly as I could and the miracle began to happen before my eyes, faster than life. The case opened, the butterfly started slowly crawling out and I shall never forget my horror when I saw how its wings were folded back and crumpled; the wretched butterfly tried with its whole trembling body to unfold them. Bending over it, I tried to help it with my breath. In vain.

It needed to be hatched out patiently and the unfolding of the wings should be a gradual process in the sun. Now it was too late. My breath had forced the butterfly to appear, all crumpled, before its time. It struggled desperately and, a few seconds later, died in the palm of my hand.

That little body is, I do believe, the greatest weight I have on my conscience. For I realize today that it is a mortal sin to violate the great laws of nature. We should not hurry, we should not be impatient, but we should confidently obey the eternal rhythm.[1]

This book is about literacy as a natural process of language acquisition. It is based upon our experiences in teaching young children. The metamorphosis of larva to butterfly is complex, even though it may appear simple to an observer. The metamorphosis of illiterate to literate is equally complex. Unlike a butterfly's development, the metamorphosis to literacy is not inevitable: The environment is not right for most children, and, of course, we are not genetically programmed to read and write. But almost all of us are genetically capable of literacy if we are

---

1. Nicholas Kazantzakis, *Zorba the Greek*, trans. by Carl Wildman (Oxford: Cassirer, 1959), pp. 129–30.

raised in a truly literate environment. Dorothy Butler's *Cushla and Her Books*[2] evidences this irrefutably.

To learn how to read and write, to become literate, children need to be taught, and then they must practice until the acts of literacy are as natural as breathing. This book is about the necessary acts of teaching, and the demands for practice if a child is to grow into literacy in a natural way. This book is also about a teacher-controlled classroom in which the teacher assumes the professional responsibility of deciding how to teach and how to demand that each child practice. Currently teachers exercise little or no control over how they teach or how the children will practice. Classrooms are dominated by legislative accountability that results in the mandating of materials and methods, and by textbook series and workbooks built to meet either their own accountability tests or those of legislators. To develop literacy, teachers must work in ways that permit children to learn effectively; they must teach so that individualization is possible through the practices prescribed. This approach needs a professional teacher—one who knows

1. What to teach
2. How to teach efficiently
3. How to get out of the way as the child practices in order to learn.

Part of teaching efficiently is knowing how to assign practices through which children learn. One of the most effective practices for learning to read is the act of reading. However, children in American schools spend most of their reading time completing Ditto sheets and workbooks and very little in the act of reading itself. Studies indicate that less than 10 percent of reading time is spent in the act of reading. A second effective practice in learning to read is to reread known material. Children who have "taught" themselves to read have all spent endless hours rereading known books. Rereading known books is rarely assigned as a task for any child.

This book has been difficult to organize. The primary reason is that books tend to be linear, presenting information in a logical, step-by-step process. Most books have some logical beginning from which additional parts flow sequentially. Our book suggests that language acquisition is not linear, that there is no first step and no particular sequence. It even suggests that attempts to make language acquisition linear are self-defeating and in fact cause much of the failure of children to learn to read and write.

2. Dorothy Butler, *Cushla and Her Books* (Boston: Horn Book, 1980).

The book is roughly organized into three parts: a statement of beliefs and theory (chapters 1–2), a description of the reading process and ways to begin the teaching of reading (chapters 3–4), and ways to write (chapters 6–9). Chapter 5 is concerned with spelling and phonics, which are part of both reading and writing. A final chapter addresses parents and nonteachers.

We approach phonics as a skill to be learned through spelling and writing and applied in reading. This approach is different, and perhaps will cause the greatest difficulty for the reader because it contains information and assumptions that are new and beliefs that are difficult to accept because they contradict much of popular belief. We find that our phonics is the last part of our approach to teaching that teachers are likely to try. Our phonics teaches children how to spell, and usually two or more months elapse before results are definitely noted. Nothing much seems to happen for a month or two, and then, as spelling is understood, there are enormous changes. We expect this, because until the child has been taught enough about print to generalize, the print system does not make sense. On the other hand, many of our suggestions about reading and writing can be taught in a day with results that are apparent immediately, and so teachers readily use them. Understanding how the phonics of our print system works is crucial to both reading and writing with excellence and ease, so that the notions expressed in chapter 5 are a fundamental part of teaching children about language and print.

We suggest that chapter 1 be read first, and probably chapter 2 should follow. Chapter 1 is tightly written, with many ideas compacted into each page. We might have extended it with examples to try to make it easier to read, but it did not seem that examples would really make it easier. Chapter 2 is simple to read, at least by comparison, and could be read first. It is not controversial, even though some of the ideas may be new. After chapters 1 and 2, there is no real sequence to the chapters. We would suggest that if any chapter seems difficult, or if part of a chapter seems difficult, it be skipped until other parts of the book have been read.

1

Literacy as Natural Learning

Oral language is universal, a characteristic of every society. Children learn to talk as a natural result of experiencing oral language. The acquisition is developmental, moving from gross approximation to sophisticated use, from immature to mature. The acquisition begins with an immersion in the cacophony of the environment as the child sorts speech from noise. The child learns from the people nearby, powerful models who are emulated in an intuitive manner. Little direct or formal teaching is done.

Speaking and listening develop naturally from this immersion in a world in which speech is the central organizer of perceptions and a central method of communication. Universally, 100 percent of children learn to speak. We believe that the potential for literacy is equally universal. Learning to read and write can and should be a normal developmental process of language acquisition, not a special achievement for an elite group, however large, nor should there be a small group of children unable to learn to read and write. However, if all children are to learn to read and write, they must be immersed in a print environment equivalent in intensity to the oral language environment from which speech emerged.

There is a visual cacophony in the child's world, a world full of people, actions, things, and print as well as oral language and noises. Children grow up in a world of labels, neon signs, billboards, pop cans, cereal boxes, records and tapes, and the advertising chaos of television. Some children grow up in an environment of newspapers, books, magazines, typewriters, word processors, and letter and note writing. Children intuitively respond to print. They sort the golden M of hamburgerland from the objects of the world, the M&Ms from the other candy labels, the *men* from *women* on the facility doors, indicating a beginning awareness that print represents things and ideas just as speech represents things and ideas. We have known children of three or four years of age who could choose without error the record they wanted played from a stack of thirty or more records. Within the stack there were several with identical labels except for the song and artist; there were some story sets in which the only distinguishing characteristic was the notation, side 1, 2, 3, or 4. These children knew which record they had but had no way of explaining how they knew. We asked, "How do you know that you have side two?" only to be met with a shrug and a smile. "Are you certain?" we pursued, only to be told assertively, "Yes!" These children could give no indication of how they knew; they just knew. As far as we could determine the children were responding intuitively to the print, not to a scratch or smudge. Responding to print occurred as naturally as responding to speech.

Literacy, however, is not universal among people or societies. Most children are not raised in a fully literate environment. For years, literacy was reserved for a select few, the leaders, priests, or merchants. Reading and writing were viewed as special, magical talents that not everyone could learn. Speaking was a primary skill learned without formal instruction by everyone; reading and writing were secondary skills based upon the oral language. Literacy skills were considered difficult to learn and to require specialized instruction, particularly for those not talented in language. This view is still present in American society and schools. Print was thought to be *speech written down*; ergo, reading was the recreating of speech, or at least reading required that individual words be pronounced as a first step in reading. This view prevails in America today so strongly that alternate views are very difficult for most people to comprehend.

There are similarities between oral and written forms within a language, but some written languages do not represent speech, and no written language is an exact representation of speech. If we teach that writing is speech written down, we may confuse children: Actually there are significant differences between speech and print. The greatest difference is the notion of the printed word—an entity set off by space on either side. Failure to grasp what a written word is causes many children great difficulty in learning to read. We speak in a continuous flow of noise, pausing only when we come to the end of a phrase or sentence, or when we run out of breath. In print, we put spaces between words. We write in a left-to-right sequence. In speech, there is no equivalent; there is no way to speak in a wrong direction. The direction in which we write seems to have been an arbitrary decision. Arbitrary decisions sometimes cause great difficulty for children who assume that some other way is the correct way. Our irregular spelling also causes children difficulty, although the problem may actually be a result of a particular teaching system that implies or tells a child to expect a phonetically regular system. Further, a child who perceives that reading is pronouncing words or requires that each word be pronounced may not learn to read: Instead of concentrating on the communication of meanings, as in acquiring speech, the child will concentrate on the saying of words. He or she even may learn to say the words without learning to read, because to learn to read one must practice reading, not word pronouncing. To learn with ease a particular language in a particular form, children must experience the language as completely and richly as possible; and they must practice with the form intensely over a long period of time.

Language without Words

There are some forms of language that have no verbal equivalents. Meanings are expressed directly without the mediation of words. Further, words may convey their equivalents only imperfectly. The written language of mathematics represents ideas that may be read directly as meanings or in whatever oral language the speaker possesses. Mime is a universal form, being read directly in whatever language the viewer possesses. Signing has some universal features that are not dependent upon a particular oral language base.

There are areas that have been labelled "nonlanguage." For example, intelligence tests commonly yield verbal or language scores and nonlanguage scores. This concept implies that certain kinds of nonverbal activities are not language and do not require language. We view these areas as nonoral forms of language akin to print. Math is one of these areas, and we have already indicated that it may be read directly as meaning. The absence of noise, utterance, is not sufficient reason to call the reading of math nonlanguage. By the same reasoning, signing would be a nonlanguage skill. Cartography, architectural drawing, and mechanical drawing, for example, are nonoral print forms of highly specialized languages that do not require a common oral base in order to be understood. They do require a commonality of form and of experiences between the producer and reader.

The arts are another area frequently thought of as nonlanguage. Again we feel this is because language is being defined too narrowly, as if words come before thoughts. Thoughts come before words, and words are merely elements of some language forms. Elliot Eisner discusses the language of art in *Reading, the Arts, and the Creation of Meaning:*

> The codes that are used in reading, in the conventional sense of the term "reading," are referred to as syntax. But syntax is not limited to the

written word. The arts, for example, possess what might be called "qualitative syntax." Qualitative syntax is the form within which a particular work is created. Abstract expressionism, surrealism, cubism, romanticism, and classicism exemplify the construction of different syntaxes in the arts "style." Each has its own logic, and each logic must be understood if the form is to be meaningfully read.[1]

Similarly, such performing arts as music and dance, theater, and film can be thought of as language forms. Each represents meanings with the intent to preserve and/or transmit ideas. Each form has structural elements that must be understood if effective communication is to take place.

Language

All languages have three characteristics:

1. Languages represent meanings.
2. Languages have functions.
3. Languages have forms with patterns or structures within each form.

These three characteristics exist concurrently or there is no language. A child immersed in a language intuits these three characteristics as part of his or her learning. A child intuits when immersed in print unless inappropriate teaching creates confusion about the function or form, reducing the act of reading or writing to a nonsense activity.

Meaning

Meaning is the most important characteristic because function and form are irrelevant without meaning. Every language represents meanings. The meanings are symbolically recorded or presented, since the meanings themselves precede the language or the need for the language. In their simplest forms, the meanings are literal, with little implied or deeper meaning. Much of language, however, is beyond the literal, and at times the literal meaning is contradicted by the deep or real meaning. *A fine kettle of fish* is neither *fine* nor *fishy*. Linguists use the terms *surface structure* and *deep structure* to label this phenomenon, and the term *semantics* refers to the branch of language study concerned with meanings. The surface level is what we are able to represent, and its origin is in

1. Elliot W. Eisner, *Reading, the Arts, and the Creation of Meaning* (Reston, Va.: National Art Education Assn., 1978), p. 18.

the deep structure within the brain. The surface structure may be speech, print, a painting, a dance, etc. but all may originate from the same deep structure of thought. For this reason, we feel that the learning of any surface structure begins with the deeper structure, the meanings that are causing the structure, and *we approach reading and writing as complementary surface structures to be learned concurrently as a form of language, not as a representation of speech to be recreated through surface-level word recognition.*

Form
Speech and print are our two most common forms of language. Every language form has some patterns or structures peculiar to the form, although there is overlap among the forms. Oral language has developed within every society, with a resulting multitude of languages with varying structures. Syntax, inflection, phoneme repetition, volume, tone, pitch, pauses, duration of sound, repetition, etc. are structural elements. Tone and pitch are not overly important in English except as an irritant or an indication of emotion or excitement. Tone and pitch are integral parts of Thai or Chinese, in which pitch denotes different meanings for sounds that are otherwise pronounced identically. Pitch is important in Spanish; three tone levels are common to both male and female speakers, while females have a fourth level which males do not use. Print is a form of language. Syntax, paragraphing, punctuation, spacing, direction of print, letters, ideographs, etc. are its structural elements. Written English uses indentation to indicate paragraphing. Thai uses extra space between lines to indicate paragraphing, a form frequently used in paragraphing American business letters. Written English uses space between words; Thai has no space between words; it leaves spaces between sentences but uses no punctuation as we use in English. Not all oral languages or all written languages use all of the elements. The elements used seem to be historical inheritances from decisions made intuitively or arbitrarily as different languages developed throughout the world.

Functions
Languages have functions. These functions may be broadly classified into three categories: (1) communicative, (2) preservative, and (3) generative. The communicative function is the obvious message giving, the transmission of ideas. Oral language has this as its main function. The preservative is the recording of ideas and thoughts so that recall is available through recreation. Writing has this function and for many years was the main way of preserving ideas and information, supplanting the oral tradition of bard, minstrel, and priest. Audiotape, videotape, film, and computers are fairly recent ways. Generative language has to do with thinking and the creation of thoughts. Initially, sensory per-

ceptions impinge upon the infant brain, and somehow thoughts are recorded within the brain's network. Through social and environmental interaction, oral language is attached to those ideas and thoughts. It is magical in that every brain does this without apparent training. It is magical in that there is no universally accepted theory or explanation for the miracle of speech. Once language has been acquired, thoughts are created that would be impossible without the language. Talking may be generative when a person is reasoning, discussing, arguing, or explaining rather than uttering words such as, "Good morning," or "How are you?" The talking creates thoughts new to the speaker. Writing is frequently generative, as any writer knows; thoughts that were not planned come into the mind through the process of transcribing planned thoughts onto paper. The act of writing itself creates thoughts.

Universally, children have demonstrated that they intuitively learn oral language easily, learning to speak in a matter of five years as well as the language is spoken around them. In later years, they mature in what they say and acquire sophistication in speaking, but the basic structures of spoken language are acquired naturally, rather effortlessly, and completely in early childhood. Children living in bilingual homes or communities acquire more than one language without seemingly being conscious that their acquisition is unusual.

Learning about Print

The learning of written language is difficult because it is difficult to immerse children in written language that has the intensity of meaning and purpose found in the oral environment. If we want to achieve universal literacy, our school goal should be to create an environment *cluttered* with print while demanding that children work with the written form. Insofar as the demand is real, the children will acquire literacy as easily as they acquired speech. This acquisition will take several years, with the learning as fraught with error as was the learning of speech. Error seems to be a symptom of language learning, not a symptom of disability. We should relate speech to print insofar as this enables the child to understand the written form. However, we must concentrate upon the communicative function and the semantic content of the written language, using print that was written to say something or to preserve ideas, not print that was devised to teach reading skills. Books that control vocabulary unnaturally, books that restrict phoneme usage, books that repeat words for the sake of word repetition make the learning of reading difficult rather than easy. Contrived books withhold portions of the real language; children need all the parts if they are to learn about print.

Reading

We sense that children who learn to read as a process of language acquisition learn in three overlapping stages:

1. Children learn that the print in books and poems is a form of language: There are messages, mysteries, and magic in books. They learn this by being read to while sitting on a lap, or they learn it when the teacher or librarian reads poems and books daily to children and repeats favorites many times. The repetition is crucial. Since the home may provide little or no lap time, schools need to accept this as their responsibility. The child learns to love books and that books are full of meaning. There is something to be comprehended and something to puzzle about in the search for greater meaning. Books are a source of joy, allowing the child unfettered forays into the unknown.

2. Children hear the same songs, poems, and stories many times; they chant, sing, and recite them to themselves. This is a natural rehearsing, done without pressure or duress. This rehearsing imprints the melodies and sounds of written English in their brains. Brains are built to discern patterns and to make sense of what impinges upon them. Each oral reading impinges on the brain, resulting finally in an imprinting of the text. With all or part of the text to look at, children begin to read along and wonder how print works. They learn about printed words by rehearsing whole passages, saying meanings first in their own oral language, later saying an author's exact words.

The idea that the reading of books occurs before the reading of words causes many people difficulty. The difficulty arises because the observation of children engaged in first reading usually occurs after the onset of school, by which time the children are either already through this stage or have been taught in such a way that this stage is occluded. The initial reading stage is akin to the stage in learning to speak when the young child is trying to communicate and cannot use sufficiently mature language to be understood. Mother clearly understands, but the neighbor or stranger cannot solve the child's utterances.

Young children who have been read to from a lap are observed universally to take books and recite from them, sometimes to a stuffed animal and at other times with no audience. They retell the story, turning the pages at appropriate times, but using their own language, saying the meanings and actions but not the exact words of the print. They will do this even from books with little or no illustration. Gradually their reading rehearsals add phrases from the story. Repeated portions, such as "'Not I,' said the cat. 'Not I,' said the dog. 'Not I,' said the mouse. 'Then I will,' said the Little Red Hen," are exactly recalled and stated. Finally, the rehearsals become so close to the exact words of the print that we might presume that the children are recognizing words. If we check, we frequently find that the children have no sense of which written words represent the individual words. We have had children who could recreate with individual word cards the exact words of a six-to-eight-line poem, nursery rhyme, or song lyric, arranging the individual words in correct sequence, but who were unable to find the word card that said *Little* or *Miss* or *Muffet* or any named word.

We sense that this stage of reading is a rehearsal, an attempt to imitate what an adult reader does orally or to solve the mystery of how print works. Although the overt manifestations may be no different from those observable in "real word recognition" reading, these children have not yet begun to focus upon the printed words as discrete entities or to apply phonics in word recognition.

3. Children learn to recognize words. They do this in many ways. The issue here is not phonics versus whole word or look-say; nor is it a matter of which of the 200 or more systems of phonics is best. Some methods of word recognition seem to be more efficient than others, but virtually all seem to work if the child has proceeded through stages one and two. The child who knows that books are about ideas, and knows the melodies of print, can learn from any system that allows one to figure out how the sounds of print work.

Typically, published reading programs in the United States reverse these three stages. Children begin by learning letters, sounds, and words, and they move into saying sentences, usually ersatz sentences written to teach reading skills, and into saying ersatz stories that contain neither mystery nor sense. The children go through the reading materials for the purpose of practicing saying words. Reading skills are taught, *mastered*, and tested before a child is expected to read trade books, real books, library books. The parts precede the whole, and the parts must be learned before the whole story or poem may be read. Word recognition is considered essential to reading. Trade books fall under the heading of enrichment and are rarely used within the teaching program, although many manuals recommend their use after the children have been taught the basic skills. This approach applied to speech would require children to master the phonemes of spoken English before allowing them to try to talk. For children who come from homes where they have had lots of lap reading and homes in which the adults use print for adult reasons, the traditional reading programs that begin with stage three seem to work reasonably well. For those children who come from homes where print is not used, there is usually confusion and frustration and frequently failure when instruction begins with stage three.

We believe that the natural way to learn written language is to begin with whole books, poems, and songs and to move to understanding and working with the parts of print. Children seem to have a natural interest in listening to poems and books read orally and a natural willingness to chant and sing. We combine this aural/oral work with writing, teaching children to write, and as part of the writing teaching phonics and spelling. Writing begins with something to say, a whole thought. The letters and words are needed, so they are taught. This integrated approach to reading and writing makes print understandable and renders true literacy accessible to all children. The understanding of the whole precedes the isolation of any bit of the language form. Reading and writing skills are a result of language acquisition, not a precursor.

Writing

American schools begin by teaching reading and presume that reading print is prerequisite to writing, except for the teaching of penmanship. There have been places, notably parts of England and much of New Zealand, where reading and writing are taught concurrently. Frequently there has been greater initial attention to writing, although the two are not separated. Children write and read what they have written and what their classmates have written—and what authors have written. The United States has rediscovered writing in the last ten years. Early writing and inventive spelling have been featured in sessions at reading-association meetings in recent years; not even minor sessions were scheduled in the 1950s and 1960s. The movement seems to have begun through English teachers rather than reading teachers, spearheaded by the work of Donald Graves in New Hampshire.

Writing seems the natural way to explore the phonics of English, the way phonics functions, and the way words are put together. People who are writing know what they want to say; therefore the meaning and wholeness exist. The noises and feelings that children extract by analyzing their own speech as they learn to spell form a natural way to understand and learn phonics. The noises and their letter representations make sense, and miraculously, they can be read by another reader even if the spelling is inventive. We teach children how to spell, and then how to spell correctly. Children learn how to recognize words if they understand how to spell and are required to write. This transfer occurs without special teaching of word-recognition skills; it occurs when children are writing fairly fluently and spelling well enough that their teacher can read their written work without difficulty.

The difference between spelling words correctly and knowing how to spell may need some explanation. Some examples of beginning spelling may help:

apl for *apple*	*fyou* for *few*
grjs for *gorgeous*	*bot* for *bought*
petesa for *pizza*	*desided* for *decided*

These are typical spellings of children beginning to solve the mystery of writing and spelling. Alphabetic spelling is simply understanding that when you say a sound you write a letter and you write the letters in the sequence that you say them, the letters moving from left to right. *Grjs* is missing the vowel representations. *Petesa, fyou,* and *desided* have some patterns in them that are incorrect for the words, but otherwise the spellings are alphabetically correct.

Writing requires a command of form or structure. Writing structures may reflect speech patterns, but much of writing is in forms not common to speech. For example, *Once upon a time* is rare in speech but common in certain children's stories. We rarely speak in rhyme, but rhyme is a common written form. There is nothing in speech to indicate paragraphing. Children can acquire dozens of writing patterns from being read to if some small attention is drawn to the patterns and if imitation of good writing is encouraged. Trade books are the best models from which to draw samples for imitation. Imitation of well-written portions of stories and poems leads to quality writing, and the practice frees children to be creative. Children sense intuitively much of what is finest in language if they are in an environment of excellent language. Print is permanent, holding language still. Imitation focuses attention so that intuition may work.

Whole-Language Teaching

Teaching begins with a content and concepts to be taught, with complete ideas and complete text. This leads to an integrated instructional program in primary grades where the language, both oral and visual, is functional. There is no step that is first; there are several first steps that occur concurrently as the child is immersed in a roomful of print. Nor is there any prescribed sequence of steps. Stories are read to children; children work with ideas in many forms expressing ideas through dance, drama, and art; letters, phonics, penmanship, and writing begin as total activities; the teacher presents whole stories orally with printed words, sentences, and some rebuses. Usually the minimum text is a full story, a complete picture book, a complete poem, a complete song lyric, or some combination of these. Occasionally the whole may be a sentence, or a label on a cereal box or pop can. Usually a word is one of the bits. Anything less than the whole text may deprive the child of the piece of the print needed to make sense. We describe Robert, who taught himself from A. A. Milne, in the next chapter. From him the whole was the four A. A. Milne books, from which he chose the four-page poem "Disobedience." We can never expect to discover what bit of language each child needs to begin or to progress; we merely must make certain that all the bits are available so that each child may individualize his or her own learning and acquire literacy.

Our problem in presenting our ideas orally or in print has always been that we cannot present everything first, nor can we provide a classroom in action in which everything is happening somewhat simultaneously. The best we can do is to ask the reader's indulgence in sensing all the parts. Particularly, we know that many teachers worry about phonics and its place in word recognition. Much of what we say in the first three chapters can be read to mean that we believe in look-say and ignore phonics. We talk about phonics in chapter 5; we believe that phonics instruction begins early, that it should be directly taught from day one in grade one, and that it is part of the word-recognition system. However, we find that our phonics makes little sense and is of little interest if presented first. We invite the reader to skim the whole book so that the bits we begin with make sense.

Our approach is not a program in the normal sense of the word. Each teacher must develop a personal program while permitting and demanding that the children work with print in useful ways. The approach accepts that language learning is social and that much of the teaching of literacy is better done with whole-class teaching than with small-group or individualized teaching. There is no series of steps that all children follow in some sequence. There are a great number of activities, that, when orchestrated by a teacher, produce literate children. This observation does not denigrate the role of the teacher; it emphasizes the importance of the teacher. It also recognizes that all learning is done individually as children practice with language and print.

2

Reading Readiness—
Extending the Lap

Early Readers

Many children come to school already reading. These early readers have been studied somewhat intensively; they have one or two common experiences. (1) Someone read to them from books. The books were available for the child to puzzle about and to practice from. (2) Someone answered their questions about print. Literacy was as natural an acquisition as speech.

Robert entered grade one reading fluently at what is typically called grade-five level. He read silently from all sorts of books and was able to retell orally what he read. His depth of comprehension was obvious, and he was able to answer all sorts of questions. He reread orally, when asked, with fluency and expression. He had been referred for evaluation by his teacher, who had noted his low score on a standardized reading readiness test and his inability to do routine readiness worksheets. She was aware that he could read well and was puzzled by the discrepancy.

We were fortunate to be able to talk with Robert, who said, "My father read me all of A. A. Milne. He read the poems over and over and I memorized them all. My favorite is 'Disobedience.' Would you like to hear it?"

> James James
> Morrison Morrison
> Weatherby George Dupree
> Took great
> Care of his Mother,
> Though he was only three. . . . [1]

1. A. A. Milne, *When We Were Very Young* (New York: Dutton, 1924), p. 30.

(Robert recited the total poem, four pages in the Milne book.) "Then I just took the book and figured out which part said what. I read all the poems over and over and then I knew the words," he said.

Robert's learning is not unique. Thousands of children have done the same thing over a period of three or four years. Robert was unique in our experience in that he knew no letter names, except *I* and *a*, which he knew as words, and *x*, which he knew as a mark for treasure maps and the like. When asked about the alphabet, the ABCs, he replied that he had heard about the alphabet but didn't know what it was. We knew Robert before the advent of "Sesame Street," which may explain why we have not met another early reader who was unconscious of the alphabet.

The Lap Technique

We have previously advocated the "lap technique."[2] It is nothing more than a loving, interested adult taking book in hand and child in lap and reading aloud. The adult does this because the sharing of books is delightful, not in order to get the child to read. This honest sharing bonds warmth, friendship, love, and caring with books. Books become part of the child's life. Books become something to be enjoyed, looked at, listened to, and responded to. The language of literature runs in and out and through the child with small silting deposits lodging in the brain with each repeated reading. The adult questions, pauses, and occasionally points to the print while reading. The child's brain gleans enough information to slowly winnow and begin to use the siftings to figure out how print works. Step one is a love of books; step two is an understanding that books have stories fraught with wonderful meanings and mysteries; step three is solving the mystery of print. Reading readiness is all of those encounters with meaning and print that comprise steps one and two and which continue as part of step three.

We infer from Robert and other early readers that the learnings of the lap technique are the essential ones in learning how to read. The child's brain seems intuitively ready to solve the mysteries of language if we begin with meaningful wholes, the whole of language and the whole of meaning.

Extending the Lap

We need to provide the learning opportunities of the lap for all children who come to school. With twenty to thirty-five children in classes we need to extend the lap. To extend the lap, we use three techniques:

---

2. Robert A. McCracken and Marlene J. McCracken, *Reading Is Only the Tiger's Tail,* 2nd ed. (Winnipeg, Manitoba: Peguis, 1986), pp. 18–20.

There was once a teeny
tiny woman who lived in a
teeny tiny house with a
teeny tiny dog and a teeny
tiny cat.

FIGURE 1. An enlarged "big book"

1. We enlarge the book, making a "big book" (fig. 1).[3] This enlargement enables all the children to discern the text.

2. We use the Weston Woods film and filmstrip versions of children's books,[4] followed by the books themselves. The films and filmstrips enlarge the pictures and train the eye to discern the picture content while listening to the text. We also use "big book" versions of the same books.

3. We create the stories or parts of stories in the pocket chart with pictures and text (fig. 2).[5] We discuss this in chapter 4.

Working from a "Big Book"

The purpose of the "big book" is to create the learnings of the lap technique with a large group. In the lap technique we begin with

3. Don Holdaway, *Foundations of Literacy* (Sidney: Ashton-Scholastic, 1978).

4. Weston Woods Studios (Canada) Ltd., 464 McNicoll Ave., Willowdale, ON M2H 2E1; Weston Woods Studios (U.S.A.) Inc., Weston, CT 06883.

5. See-through pocket chart as designed and developed by Marlene J. McCracken; manufactured in Canada and the United States by School Arts Materials, P.O. Box 45162, Seattle, WA 98145.

FIGURE 2. A pocket chart

children less than a year old and give them the leisure of four or five years to learn about print. Five- and six-year-olds can assimilate these learnings much more quickly because we direct their attention to critical print features. To do this we follow a seven-step recipe. We do only the first two steps in kindergarten and all seven in grade one.

1. We read the "big book" with the whole class, allowing the children to see the pictures and savor the hearing. We encourage the children to join in the oral reading of repeated parts:

> "Not I," said the cat.
> "Not I," said the dog.
> "Not I," said the mouse.
> "Then I will," said the little Red Hen. And she did.

We pause occasionally to allow the children to fill in a word or phrase, just as we would with a single child on our lap. We track with our finger, indicating each word in a natural motion so that the children's attention begins to focus on the print. The tracking should not be used for the first reading.

2. We choose some part to read with particularly dramatic intonation, trying various inflections to indicate various moods or messages. For example the question, *"My, what have you been eating, my little cat? You are so fat!"* is repeated numerous times in Jack Kent's telling of *Fat Cat.*[6] We point to the words as we model various intonational emphases: first, "My, what have you been EATING . . . ," then, "My, what HAVE you been eating . . . ," and "MY, WHAT have YOU been eating . . . ," etc. We have the children read with us and then echo the lines alone.

3. We do the remaining steps with small groups of children, usually eight at a time with a random mix of abilities in each group. We read aloud, pointing to each word, keeping our reading natural. We read normally in meaningful phrases with dramatic intonation; the children echo the part we have read. We read a full clump of meaning, usually a full sentence and sometimes two or three sentences if they are short. We say:

MY TURN:	Once upon a time a little red hen was raking her yard when she found a grain of wheat.
YOUR TURN:	[The group of eight respond in unison as the teacher points to the words. Their reading is a normal cadence modeled after the teacher's, not word by word.]
MY TURN:	"Who will help me plant the wheat?" said the Little Red Hen.

6. Jack Kent, *The Fat Cat* (New York: Parents Magazine Pr., 1971).

YOUR TURN: [The children repeat as the teacher tracks.]
MY TURN: "Not I," said the dog. "Not I," said the cat. "Not I," said the mouse. "Then I will," said the Little Red Hen. And she did.
YOUR TURN: [The children repeat.]

We read five to ten pages or the whole story, depending upon the amount of text on each page. We do this many times if the children are not responding in a manner that indicates they have good control of the story. This may take several days.

4. We teach from one page at a time and focus upon the individual words, one word at a time. Each session we ask the children to find several words—*hen, once, dog, mouse, wheat, found,* etc. We use small chalkboards (twelve by eighteen inches). We tell the children to locate the word *hen* with their eyes and to copy it on the chalkboard. They all work at the same time. Many children have difficulty copying, so we teach them to focus on the whole word. We spell the word together chanting the letter names until they can write the word without looking. Copying letter by letter, looking back each time, is unproductive and many children spend time frustrated trying to locate and relocate the word they are copying.

We put a full sentence on word cards, one word per card, and tell the children that we have some puzzles for them to solve. Sometimes alone and sometimes in groups, the children are given a set of cards and asked to make sense out of it. If necessary we tell them what the cards say. Many children need help initially in knowing what the cards are supposed to say. The children sequence the cards. We do this for several sentences, and sometimes the pupils take two or three sentences and sequence them.

We print the whole story on sentence strips, putting a meaningful phrase or complete sentence on each card. We use the shorter "big book" stories for this exercise, stories with less than 300 words. We pass out all the sentence strips so that each child has at least one. We ask, "Who has the beginning of the story?" and the child places it in the top pocket of the pocket chart. We continue building, letting the children read and reread as they use phonics to determine if they have the next phrase.

5. Buddy pairs do oral reading of a page of the story. Sometimes each pair has two pages. They need to have a chunk of the story to read and practice with. Each pair has a different page of the story, and the buddies read orally together, pointing to the words as they read. The teacher monitors the four pairs, helping only as necessary. Usually the buddies help each other. They read their pages until they have practiced

about three to five minutes. (We use unbound copies of "big books" for this exercise.)

6. Now the text is read orally in the story sequence, with each pair reading the part they have practiced. Steps 4, 5, and 6 are repeated until the whole story has been practiced. The whole story is now shuffled, and the children sequence the pages. We make most of our books without page numbers, so that the children will not use the numbers for sequencing.

7. Now we have made the book accessible to the children so that they are able to read the whole story from the small trade book. The book, in multiple copies, has been available in the room library throughout the whole cycle and many children have already read it many times. However, as step seven, we now demand that the children practice from the trade book many times. Children practice naturally when they sense that they are learning and have a real story to read. This is what children of the home lap technique have done at leisure, and we must demand this of grade ones who come to school without it.

This is whole-to-part teaching. We begin with a complete story, and we gradually move to the parts, the sentences, the phrases, the words, and finally the letters. This assures that each child has the chance to understand the parts and bits; with repeated experiences the parts make sense. With sense comes memorization, a memorization as natural as the memorization of the words of speech.

Working from Poems and Songs

Similarly we use songs and poems. Step one is oral. We recite or sing together until the lyric is memorized over a period of days.

Step two is to attend to the words. The lyric is printed in large print on butcher paper or tag board and hung in view. Or we use "big book" or the pocket chart (fig. 3). We may use the print in learning the lyric in step one. We frequently use rebuses in learning songs or poems.

Step three repeats the copying on the chalkboards and the recreating with sentence strips or word cards.

We make lots of songs into "big books," nine by twelve or twelve by eighteen inches, with large print and pictures, usually with one lyrical phrase per page. The books are not bound. Once a song has been memorized, children shuffle the pages and put them back in order. This is a favorite activity of children who are solving the mysteries of print.

We print our song and poem lyrics on rolls of butcher paper or wallpaper, writing from bottom to top. We leave lots of space between words, rarely putting more than two words on a line. We unroll the roll

FIGURE 3. *"Good Morning to the Sun" in the pocket chart*

on the floor, and one child walks the words as the class sings or recites. Of course, children also do this alone and love the practice. We cover our songs with a plastic rug runner, which permits us to see through and protect the words so that many, many children can walk and recite. Kindergarten children love to try to do this even though they are just discovering what a word is; first-grade children choose this as a free-time activity. All seem to like to do the walking, as evidenced by their choosing to walk the words in the hall on their way to the cafeteria, bus, or library.

There are many songbooks published as trade books. Many are currently in print. Most have delightfully large pictures. Only a few have large print. We can easily enlarge the print on a chart or on pocket-chart strips once we have taught the song from the picture book.

Sustained Silent Reading—A Rehearsal Time

With kindergarten and grade one we use a variation of *sustained silent reading* (SSR) that provides a lap for those children who cannot use books independently. SSR is a time during which everyone in the room reads silently. With beginners *silent* is a misnomer; it means that each child reads independently and expects that no one is paying attention to the oral reading that usually emanates.

Sustained silent reading for beginners is not successful unless they know lots of stories and know some stories well enough to recite them pretty much from memory. In kindergarten children do lots of looking at books all at the same time, but SSR is more than looking at books. It is attending to stories and ideas, and of course the learning of words as a result. The teacher needs to read ten to twenty books to children, and the books need to be reread orally and discussed several times. After gaining fairly good command of a story it is natural for the child to take the book alone and to rehearse reading, retelling the story from the stimulation of both picture and text. Initial rehearsals are usually only approximations of the actual text, and usually they reflect the text exactly only in repeated lines such as, "Not by the hair of my chinny-chin-chin!"or the, "I don't care!" of *Pierre*.

The teacher explains SSR to the children, saying, "We are all going to read to ourselves for the next five or ten minutes. We will each select a book, and we will read it to ourselves and not bother anyone else." The teacher makes certain that every child has a book, and makes particularly certain that the children least experienced with literature have one of the books that has been presented several times. Now everyone begins, and the teacher reads intently from some adult book or magazine. We sometimes introduce catalogs for children to read, particularly Christmas toy catalogs. If everyone reads well enough, the time elapses without the teacher doing anything but reading. Often, however, after five or six minutes some children will seem finished with their books, and the teacher may say, "If you would like to bring your books up close I'll read some of them quietly to you." If reading aloud has been done every day, we find that only five to ten children accept this invitation. Insofar as possible, this becomes a snuggle and read-to time, where the child whose book is being read is the closest. Two or three books get read this way. Sometimes the teacher reads only part of several books during this time, asking the children to pick their favorite two pages for reading. Since all the books have already been read orally many times, the reading of only a portion seems acceptable to the children.

Most kindergarten and many grade-one children are not reading during SSR in the adult sense of the word. SSR in kindergarten and grade one is really a rather noisy time, but no one is paying attention to the noise that accompanies the silent reading. Most children begin reading orally; to them silent reading merely means that no one is listening. It is not the noise that makes this nonadult reading. Most children are rehearsing; they are saying the stories aloud to themselves while looking at the pages, sometimes at the words, and sometimes even trying to find the right words to match the memorized text. When they are trying to find the words they usually point. This is not to be discouraged. Pointing drops out automatically once it is no longer needed in order to find where the individual words are. They work independently, and frequently for extended periods beyond the SSR time, reciting and rehearsing. They work from known materials usually, but they also read the way many children of three to five read when given the chance to sit on the library or bookstore floor with an unknown picture book. They create an oral story based upon the pictures, or they comment about the pictures without any story line to hold the observations in place.

3

Reading as Apprehension and Prediction

Thus far we have described inducting children into reading without defining or describing the process other than alluding to it as an intuitive language-learning process. Reading has to do with apprehension. The meanings and the intuited melodies of written language stored in the brain act to direct the eyes to see upon the page what the brain expects should be there.

Using Predictable Materials with No Unknown Concepts

We can demonstrate anticipation using a simple story, *The Farmer and the Skunk*.[1] The reader's job is to fill in the words:

> The skunk sat under the porch.
> The farmer sat on _____ _____.
> The skunk smelled the farmer.
>
> _____ _____ _____ _____.
>
> The skunk saw _____ _____.
>
> _____ _____ _____ _____.
>
> The skunk got on the porch.
>
> _____ _____ _____ _____ _____.
>
> The skunk got off the porch.
> The farmer got on the table.
>
> _____ _____ _____ _____ _____ _____.
> _____ _____ _____ _____ _____ _____.
> _____ _____ _____ _____ _____ _____.

1. Robert A. McCracken and Marlene J. McCracken, *The Farmer and the Skunk* (San Rafael, Calif.: Leswing Pr., 1972; Winnipeg, Manitoba: Peguis, 1986).

More than likely you have just thought or said, "The skunk got off the table," completing eighteen consecutive words of reading without seeing a single word. You can do this for two reasons. You have the structures of English in your brain; intuitively you recognized the chase, the noun, verb, and prepositional phrase structure of this simple story. You also know enough about skunks to know that a person would take some kind of avoiding action. As soon as you read the next line of the story, "The farmer got in the truck," you can complete the next three sentences without error. With a little bit of meaning from the author, you bring to bear upon print an apprehension that enables you to predict the meanings that will occur, and in simple, structured writing the exact words that the author is likely to use.

With more mature books you apprehend the ideas that you may meet; you look at the print to find what words the author used and so discover whether you predicted correctly. Comprehension becomes more an affirmation of apprehension than a pronouncing of words to discover meaning. This does not explain how a reader comprehends material that is not apprehended, except to imply that without apprehension no reading occurs. This explains why fantasy fails when it goes too far beyond reality; it becomes incomprehensible. We are all familiar with the puzzlement of being able to say each word in a paragraph or sentence without understanding. Directions for assembling a Christmas toy fall into this category. I can, for example, read aloud the following directions to my wife, who can follow them easily:

> Using size 2¾ mm. needles, cast on 112 sts.
> and work 26 rows of k.l, p.l rib, inc. 1 st.
> at end of last row on 2nd, 4th, 6th, and 8th.
> sizes only.

I have only the vaguest notion what I have pronounced because I have never knitted from a pattern. I know the abbreviations, so that I can say glibly, "Using size two and three-quarter millimeter needles, cast on one hundred twelve stitches and work twenty-six rows in knit one, purl one ribbing, increasing one stitch at the end of the last row on the second, fourth, sixth, and eighth sizes only."

If you were able to understand the directions it is because you have some knitting knowledge already stored in your brain, knowledge gained from knitting before you could read about knitting. Without such knowledge, the pronouncing of words does not result in reading.

From my eleven-year-old daughter's books I can read orally:

> Arabians are small horses. Most are between 14.1 and 15.1 hands tall. The height is always taken from the ground to the top of the withers.

She has comprehension. I don't know an Arabian from any other breed by sight, and I comprehend only that I measure from the ground, hardly satisfactory comprehension.

I could choose technical or scientific material to make the same point, but these excerpts would likely include polysyllabic terms, making the difficulty seem to be a problem of words. To read I have to have sufficient information already stored in my brain so that I may apprehend. Relevant meaning already resides in me, or I am unlikely to be able to read a particular bit of print. When a book is too difficult for a child to read, it usually means that the child needs help with understanding the content represented by the text, even when the child is unable to read the text orally. Meaning is the basis for all language understandings. Too often we help the poor reader with the form only.

It is unlikely that any reader read the passage from *The Farmer and the Skunk* quoted at the beginning of this chapter as follows:

> [The farmer got on the table.]
> The skunk got on the table.
> The farmer got off the table.
> The skunk got off the table.
> *The farmer*

You did not think *The farmer* because the words are meaningless. We think *meanings*, and we read *meanings*, not *words*. It is equally unlikely that any reader was surprised by the story continuing with *The farmer*. As soon as you read *The farmer got in the truck*, you will be able to continue reading _____ _____ _____ ____ _____ _____. You read when you have anticipatory meaning; you read with apprehension. You recognize the words that appear on the page quickly, effortlessly, because they are the words that you expect to see. You have projected meaning onto the page. You do not sound out each word, and you do not consciously recognize each word to get the meaning. Meaning dominates word recognition. For example, when reading a story about deer, the sentence *Both fawns froze when the does barked,* is read without puzzlement about the pronunciation of *does*. *Does* in isolation, however, will almost always be pronounced as *duz*, with *doughs* never thought of. *Fawns* creates an expectation for *doughs* and the brain unconsciously apprehends and confirms that the *does barked*.

With beginning readers we must develop the expectation of what the print will say. We must develop an intuitive expectation for written English syntax. Without the melodies of written English in you, you would not have been able to read *The Farmer and the Skunk*. This is what lap reading does. (Note you read *duz*.) Lap reading develops an expectation for meaning and for syntax. This is what chanting, singing, rereading orally, "big book" work, storytelling from the pocket chart, etc. do. They set into the child's brain an anticipation, an expectation, an apprehension of the exact words that will appear on the page, in the pocket chart, in the "big book," in the song lyric, etc. The child now looks with eyes that expect to find specific words—words that somehow get learned by meaningful repetition.

It is here that the child begins to apply phonics, phonics which we have been teaching through spelling. The child knows that it is either the farmer's or the skunk's turn; the child anticipates that the farmer should begin with an *f* and skunk with an *s*, and with the cooperation of expectation and peripheral vision the word *farmer* or the word *skunk* is recognized. Phonics is part of the anticipatory set. Words should look something like we expect them to look. Most do, and so long as we do not expect the words to be absolutely as expected, the variations do not disturb our reading and our learning of the words. In this approach to reading, the recognition of words in isolation is a final step or a symptom that the brain has learned the printed form of a particular word.

Sylvia Ashton-Warner in *Teacher* develops the notion of organic learning.[2] She describes introducing Maori children to print, something foreign to many of them. She developed key words, one-look words, and writes that if you choose powerful enough words, words with sufficient organic meaning, the children learn the print form forever with one look, with a single exposure to the word in print. The taboo nature of many of the words learned by the Maori children seems to have obscured her findings for some people. The children learned words relating to sex, and words such as *love, jail,* and *kill.* They learned these words without knowing the names or the sounds represented by the letters. They learned them because their brains already held such powerful meanings for those words that the abstraction of print was assimilated in one look. Our work with children would support Ashton-Warner. We find that when we can develop intense meaning for words, those words are learned quickly and retained seemingly forever. American children come to school with thousands of oral words but with very few of intense meaning. We have found that we must develop meaning if we want children to learn and retain words easily. Perhaps our best American evidence is the learning of *Tyranosaurus rex, triceratops, pteradactyl,* and other dinosaur words by children who seemingly are having difficulty in learning to read.

Cloze Technique for Building Apprehension and Comprehension

We use a version of the cloze technique to develop vocabulary, apprehension, and phonics. This is merely taking a story or text paragraph and

2. Sylvia Ashton-Warner, *Teacher* (New York: Simon & Schuster, 1965).

deleting several words. We choose the deletions carefully so that we can develop apprehension for whatever part of the language we may wish to emphasize, although usually we develop several parts at one time. For cloze to work successfully in developing apprehension there must be sufficient text to have a clear context, and the content must be familiar. We delete no more than one word for every ten words of text within any selection, although we may have two deletions separated by only a word. For younger children we tend to have even more text. For example:

> People said that the old woman who lived in the _____ was strange. She never went into the village, and she kept to herself. She must be very _____, that woman, and she always was different. Some said that she was a _____, but whether she was or she _____, she was scary, and nobody would go near her.[3]

We tell the children to read the whole paragraph silently, and then we point to the first blank and ask them what word might go into the space. Often we read the whole paragraph together orally following the silent reading before we brainstorm. We list on the chalkboard all the words we can think of for space one. As we list the words we sometimes write a letter, such as *c* and say, "I am thinking of a word that begins with *c*" and try to elicit additional words, such as *cave, cavern,* or *cabin.* We are not concerned with getting the word that the author used although it is very unlikely that it will not be elicited. We elicit for the second space, and then the rest, trying to get thirty or more words for each space. Some spaces, however, such as the last one here, will accommodate only one response if we allow only one word, *wasn't.* Finally we read each of the sentences in the story orally, in unison, to test how each word sounds and to see if each of the brainstormed words makes sense. In brainstorming we take almost every response without comment and check for meaning and sound afterwards.

The purpose of the exercise is not to learn the words by sight, nor to get the author's word and learn it. It is to develop first an apprehension for a suitable meaning that can be represented by a word or a number of words and, with most words, to develop some sense of apprehension of how they should be spelled. We do develop paragraph meaning by talking about the shades of meaning that various word choices create, asking children to choose the best words to create a scary story, the best words to create a funny story, the best words to create a peaceful story, etc.

With this story, the teacher might continue by showing two or three of the illustrations and having the children predict which words the

3. Marta Koci, *Blackie and Marie* (New York: Morrow, 1981), p. 1.

author might have used in the opening paragraph. Then the actual opening paragraph is read to the children, followed by predicting what may happen in the story. If the teacher reads the next two pages, the predictions will become much more accurate. The teacher should then read the whole story without further interruption. The value in prediction is not in being correct; the value is in developing an anticipatory attitude toward print. Things predicted correctly are easily understood and remembered; surprisingly, things not predicted correctly are also more easily understood and remembered.

Cloze technique develops word-attack skills while focusing upon comprehension, so that both word-attack skills and comprehension improve. Children come to treat an unknown visual form as a problem in meaning. The list of words developed for any one blank explores the meanings that were available to an author. With meaning established, the pupils use phonics to determine which word of a restricted list the author may have used. It is this establishment of meaning prior to the application of phonics that enables the reader to read the word *does* as *duz* or *doughs* without consciously considering the wrong pronunciation, or to differentiate between heteronyms such as *wind in the trees* and *wind the yarn,* which requires peripheral vision to the right of the word *wind* to solve the puzzle fluently. More important this technique teaches the child to read and to learn to identify the word that belongs in the blank. For example:

> The sun was shining. The temperature was 75 degrees. The food was piled on the table. It was a _____ day for the school picnic.

Presume that the child does not know the visual form of the word that appears in the blank in the actual book. The context dictates that the meaning be pleasant. The context will not accommodate *horrible, rotten,* or *miserable.* The context restricts the list of possible words to *wonderful, lovely, tremendous, gorgeous, exceptional,* etc. If the word is *gorgeous* the soft *g* instead of a *j* in the middle and *eous* spelling of *us* cause the brain no difficulty in solving the mystery quickly because *gorgeous* is the only word of the group that has the expectation of *g* at the beginning, *r* somewhere in the middle and *s* on the end. If there are two words of like meaning having similar phonetic expectation, the child is likely to miscall the word if reading orally, or to just read on silently with no diminution of comprehension or fluency. All of this occurs quite automatically without the brain being distracted from comprehending by undue attention to phonic rules or peculiarity of spelling. For example, grade-one children frequently substitute *house* for *home* and vice versa until they have had sufficient practice with print to have learned the words more automatically. This occurs even though they know *house* and *home* on a word list without error. Since a word list has no context, it cannot be read; the words can only be pronounced, so greater attention to the detail is required.

We select most of our cloze paragraphs from books that we are teaching from, so that the content that we develop is related to what we are teaching. Sometimes we create a paragraph that forces attention to a particular concept that we wish to develop. The cloze exercises build readiness for the content that children will be reading and build reading skills through the content. Cloze exercises done in isolation, divorced of content needs, develop skill in doing exercises, and the skill rarely transfers to other reading.

Apprehension and Prediction in Reading Novels

We use another form of prediction to read novels with children, using novels as "big books." The activity works well from grade three on and may be used successfully with some grade-two classes. We work with the whole class for this activity. We transcribe the first page, or the first 150 words, of each chapter of a novel onto overhead transparencies. We tell the children the title and author of the book, usually putting both on the chalkboard. We project page 1 of chapter 1 and tell the pupils to read it silently. We then ask questions to probe their understandings. We sometimes point to key words or character names before we tell them to read silently to make sure that certain words are pronounced correctly. We do all sorts of comprehension questioning to develop the literal and inferential meaning on the page, and then we probe for what seems to be coming on the next page and the following several pages. We push for sensible, logical answers. We ask children to explain their predictions. By doing this we are asking children to tell other children something of the mental processes they are using as they read. We are getting children to think; and we are getting them to apprehend by developing questions that they know the story answers. *We accept all answers and do not push for the "right" answer. Pushing for a right answer changes the purpose from sharing predictions, a thinking activity, to outwitting the teacher, a game.*

The final step is to read in unison, following the teacher's pointer as it tracks the text. This tracking is done so that the choral reading is natural and fluent, with pauses at periods and commas. This gives the child who is having difficulty in word recognition a chance to locate the exact words of the author after having listened to the meanings as they were developed in the oral work. This approach is consistent with the notion that we should develop the ideas that will appear on the page before we attend to the exact words. This procedure becomes our in-class remedial reading program and English as a second language program.

Next we project the beginning of chapter 2, checking our predictions and changing those that obviously need changing because we now have additional information. We repeat the whole process, first reading silently, then discussing fully with lots of teacher questioning, projecting to the beginning of chapter 3, etc., until we have finished the book. (We have projected, read, and discussed less than 10 percent of the text.) This activity takes fifty minutes or more and sometimes requires sessions on two consecutive days. We find virtually no flagging of interest if we have chosen an exciting book that is reasonably predictable, even though the lesson is long and sustained. The most common response when we finish is the demand to hear the whole story, or a plea by almost everyone to be allowed to read the book alone. We try to have five or more copies of the book available because every child wants to try to read the story.

We have used *The Sword in the Tree* by Clyde Robert Bulla.[4] The first page of chapter 1 is as follows:

Weldon Castle
1

The boy sat up in bed. A sound in the night had wakened him.

His room was so dark he could see nothing, but he could hear steps outside his door. He held his breath and listened.

"Shan!" said a voice.

He let his breath go. It was his mother, calling his name.

"Yes?" he said. "What is it?"

Lady Marian came into the room. She had a candle in her hand, and the light moved over the stone walls.

"Shan, I'm glad to find you here," she said. "I was afraid you had gone with your father."

Sometimes we begin merely asking the pupils, "What is happening?" and then base our questions upon their answers. Other times we begin with a pointed question such as, "What time is it?" The obvious answer is *night,* but we follow this by asking what time at night, pushing to get a definite hour and then asking why. Pupils generally set some time after midnight and are rarely able to give a reason why except that they feel this strongly. We accept this kind of intuitive certainty but we push them to explain. Intuitive certainty is a characteristic of many able readers. They feel confident that their inferences are right, but we want them to begin to understand their intuitions, and we want them to talk about the way in which they think so that other children can gain insight into ways of thinking about text.

We deal quickly with the literal meaning on the page and then we push pupils to project backward, even though this is page one. We want

---

4. Clyde Robert Bulla, *The Sword in the Tree* (New York: Crowell, 1957).

to establish that some sort of message arrived and that father left hurriedly, indicating that there is some sort of emergency. We push children to project forward into the next paragraph and the next several pages. We have had children who speculated that Shan was awakened by the drawbridge lowering and that father has gone off to war. There is no way of proving this, but the child who explains the theory to the class is clearly defining one part of reading as bringing meaning and pictures to the printed page. Father has not gone off to war, but the speculation is reasonable and will lead the reader on sensibly.

As a final step page 1 of chapter 1 is read orally as the teacher points. Then the first page of chapter 2 is projected for silent reading.

Uncle Lionel

2

Shan had heard many tales of his uncle. Now he wanted to hear more. "Tell me about my Uncle Lionel," he said to his father.

"Wait until he is strong," said Lord Weldon, "and he will tell you himself."

Shan asked his mother, "Will you tell me about my uncle?"

"I never knew him well," she said. "He sailed from England long before you were born. He was wild when he was a boy. He was never a kind and gentle knight, and he was never as brave as your father."

"Did he live here at Weldon Castle?" asked Shan.

We now check our predictions regarding "Where had father gone?" Now we usually agree that he had gone to get his brother, who was wounded. "Might he just have been sick?" we ask, and the pupils sense that a rescuing emergency had taken place, not mere help to a sick brother who needed convalescence. We question why mother is worried about Uncle Lionel's arrival and establish the sense of foreboding. We ask, "What kind of tales has Shan heard?" We develop some understanding of the form of the novel, too. Grade-five and grade-six children recognize Lionel's role in the story if asked what he is going to do. They reply that he is going to cause trouble. To understand Uncle Lionel's function in the story—without the formal label *antagonist*—is to begin to understand one type of novel. We teach so that children can apprehend and read this particular book, but we also use the teaching to develop an understanding of form so that apprehension is even better. We ask, "Is Uncle Lionel going to recover?" and frequently get the answer, "He has to if he is going to cause trouble," which indicates that at least some children have intuitively understood the form. We read orally together.

Now we project the first page of chapter 3:

The Oak Tree

3

The next day Lionel asked to be taken outside.

"I want to sit in the shade of the great oak tree," he said.

The oak tree stood in the castle garden. There were some who said it was the oldest tree in all England. Ever since Shan was a small boy, he had liked to climb it. High in its trunk he had found a hollow so large that he could nearly get inside it.

"I fear the oak will die, with such a large hollow in its trunk," Lord Weldon had said.

But the tree was still strong and green, and each spring it put out new leaves and branches.

Four servants carried Lionel, bed and all, into . . .

We ask, "Is Lionel getting better?" "What is Shan going to do now that his uncle is sitting in the garden?" Sometimes we have to reproject chapter 2 to elicit the guess that Shan will now have the chance to ask his uncle about his adventures. We tell the pupils that Clyde Robert Bulla is a fine author who does not waste words. And we ask, "Why does he interrupt the story to talk about the hole in the oak tree?" Sometimes we have to refer to the book title to stimulate the responses. "What sword will be in the tree? Why do you think it will be there? Who might put it there?" We push this very directly because the denouement of this story needs this apprehension. Again we finish by reading the page orally in unison.

Sword in the Tree has fourteen chapters. We read one page from each chapter and we make numerous predictions. We confirm some, disaffirm some, and raise lots of questions that go unanswered. By the end of the book, the pupils' brains are full of unanswered questions, which they carry with them into the reading of the novel. They frequently do not begin with the first chapter but seek out the chapter that seems most likely to answer their most compelling questions. They usually read the whole book. The process in one way is akin to the behavior of excellent readers as a teacher reads an entire book orally. Avid readers reread the whole book individually after the teacher finishes the oral reading. This process eliminates many word-recognition problems within the story; all of the proper names have been pronounced several times, and the understandings have been developed so that the story line can be followed even with weak word-recognition skills. The first page of each chapter has been rehearsed fully enough so that at least those pages can be practiced successfully. A child who meets difficulty can always skip and find a part that can be read successfully. The procedure allows teachers to demand that the poorer readers do what good readers already do, practice reading by reading familiar stories. Good readers read lots of books more than once, gaining skill, increased comprehension, and enjoyment through the rereading. Poor readers rarely have the time or the inclination to read something twice, nor do they have the apprehensive set that enables them to do sustained reading of stories and novels or materials that are reasonably mature. Reading is the recreation of an author's meanings, meanings that have been apprehensively developed prior to the viewing of the print. Word recognition comes about much as it did with *The Farmer and the Skunk* except that the reader uses an already established sight vocabulary and cloze approach to unknown words, with phonics confirming which words the author used to express a particular meaning.

We draw attention to the parts of a novel—plot, mood, character development—noting that Lionel is the *bad guy*, the one who will cause trouble. Whether we teach the name *antagonist* as fitting Lionel's role depends upon the maturity of the class. We are in no rush to teach labels; we are most concerned with developing concepts. Once a concept is firmly understood, the label is easy to attach, and we want to avoid verbalism that gives children the appearance of understanding.

Choosing novels for this sort of reading is tricky. Not all authors say enough at the beginning of the chapter to make this sort of prediction feasible. Some authors say their most important ideas at the end of the chapter, some spread the predictive pages throughout, and some are not consistent. We have successfully used the chapter ends of some novels and selected pages of others, focusing on some portion of each chapter and using approximately 150 words.

However, we have found a way that helps in choosing. The teacher selects a book that he or she has not read, and reads only the beginning of each chapter. If the teacher can predict, children are likely to be able to do so, too. Now the teacher reads the whole book to determine its general suitability. Reading the whole novel also permits the teacher to question the students specifically, so that the range of responses is narrowed, and to make certain that clues to significant themes are recognized. In *Sword in the Tree*, Nappus, one of the Weldon servants, writes in the ashes. It is important several chapters later that the pupils realize that Nappus is mute. The first pages of the chapters do not make this obvious, but children will predict this as one of the possible reasons if they are pushed for several answers to the question, "Why did Nappus write in the ashes instead of whispering?"

This technique is relatively new, but it seems to be a compelling way to develop the anticipatory set and questioning attitude that book readers have. The enlarged print seems to enable pupils to follow along, keeping their place without difficulty. It also seems to make the details of print discernible. Our observations with five- and six-year-old children have led us to believe that some children do not even see book print as print. We speculate that they see an undiscriminated mass of squiggles as decoration. Many children who have worked with large print have stated abruptly when looking at normal print, "Oh! This is the same as the 'big book' (or pocket chart)!" They had never seen the normal page of print as print, and so of course they never could solve the trick of reading. It is possible that the use of enlarged print enables them to focus upon the significant features of print in learning to solve the problem of word recognition. We have found many older children having difficulty with reading who did not understand the concept of a written word or the notion of alphabetic writing. The enlarged print and choral reading with tracking seem to help.

With this technique we have seen startling success for poor readers who have not progressed with individual remedial work. They become alive and attentive, and they learn when immersed in the work of the total class, while struggling to read novels that everyone is working with. It may be merely the psychological relief of working on class material rather than special or babyish material. However, we think that this method succeeds because reading is redefined as a questioning, predicting, answer-seeking activity, rather than a word recognition activity, and books are made accessible for practice. We feel certain that the oral work provides a linguistically full environment free of correction or embarrassment for children who are learning English as a second language. We need only observe the pupil involvement when a novel is presented this way to know that the technique is effective in keeping almost every child constantly working.

4

Beginning Reading from the Pocket Chart

One way to introduce children to print with instant success is to teach them from materials that are predictable within themselves or predictable because the children have memorized the text. Children who come to reading naturally without formal instruction learn to recognize words by looking at memorized materials and figuring out which words and which letters say what.

It is natural for children to practice with materials if they are learning from the material. Drill is natural. There is no particular need for duress or reward. Learning is the brain's natural reward, an activity that needs no extrinsic motivation or reward if it is meaningful. Children usually treat such practice as play. It may seem that they are doing what they enjoy and that their play is causing the learning. However, we believe that it is the learning that causes the pleasure, and that we should use pleasure as a sign that a child is learning, not as a precursor for drill. If we read children a book such as *The Farmer and the Skunk*,[1] they take it and rehearse, rereading again and again, individually and in small groups, reading together and to each other. The words *the, on, off* become implanted in the brain. The implantation is slower than for *skunk*, a word that seems to have intense meaning for most children and is learned virtually instantly.

Many stories can be told orally and the print presented and taught in the pocket chart. We will describe the use of some books in detail and suggest others that can be taught similarly. We have undoubtedly omitted many excellent books. The rule in using books with children is to choose books that you personally enjoy.

1. Robert A. McCracken and Marlene J. McCracken, *The Farmer and the Skunk* (San Rafael, Calif.: Leswing Pr., 1972; Winnipeg, Manitoba: Peguis, 1986).

The complete text of some stories can be presented; with others only a portion is used, focusing upon some repeated parts that the teacher and children read together chorally. Some books build up the chart, beginning at the bottom and adding lines upward; some books are built down, beginning with the first line. There is no particular sequence in choosing stories or techniques. All books are print sources from which children can learn about print. Books with limited print, however, may make learning about print more difficult. Too little print may provide insufficient information for the child to generalize; too much may overwhelm. We work with a wide range of materials and carefully observe the responses of the children and use their responses to guide our teaching. Regardless, the books must be natural language with full literary richness.

Six Steps in Beginning Reading

We use six steps in teaching stories to kindergarten and first-grade children. Step one is not completed before beginning step two, nor is step two completed before step three. All six are done many times with many stories. We use all of the six simultaneously for children in grades two and above who are still beginning to read or for children in grade one who have begun reading. The steps flow together, and we do as many of them as the children can handle. We individualize the practices and drills so that within one class individual children may be practicing at step one, two, three, four, five, or six. We do mostly step one in kindergarten, rarely getting formally into step two until late in the kindergarten year.

Step One: The Children Memorize the Story
Sometimes merely repeated oral reading is enough for children to memorize a story. Usually we help children memorize the exact words of a story by giving them picture clues. The classic old tale, *The Old Woman and Her Pig,*[2] builds easily up the pocket chart.

> An old woman was sweeping her house when she found a little crooked sixpence.
> [We put a picture of the old woman's house in the bottom of the chart, and read on. See fig. 4a.]

> "What should I do with this sixpence?" she said to herself. "I know. I will go to market and buy a little pig."

---

2. Anne Rockwell, *The Old Woman and Her Pig, and Ten Other Stories* (New York: Crowell, 1979).

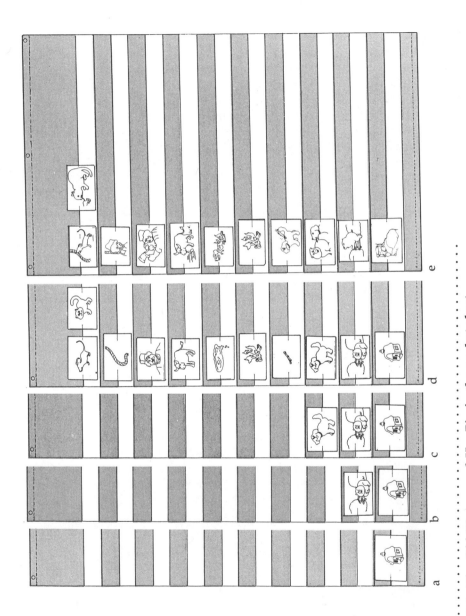

FIGURE 4. **The Old Woman and Her Pig in the pocket chart**

As she was coming home, she came to a stile, but piggy wouldn't go over the stile. [See fig. 4b.]
[We put a picture of piggy in front of the stile in the next line of the pocket chart and read on.]

She went a little farther and she met a dog.
[We insert a picture of a dog and read on. See fig. 4c.]

"This dog can be a help to me," she thought. So she said, "Dog, dog! Bite pig! Piggy won't go over the stile, and I shan't get home tonight." But the dog wouldn't.
[We point to each picture as we chant.]

We continue reading, adding the stick, the fire, the water, the ox, the butcher, the rope, the rat, and the cat, one picture at a time. (See fig. 4d.) With each added picture we point to all the pictures and have the children chant the accumulating repeated parts. Once we have fed milk to the cat we all chant the "began to" parts: "The cat began to kill the rat; the rat began to gnaw the rope," etc. (See fig. 4e.) We show this by turning over the cards that have the "began to" action sequences on the other side. On one side is the cat, and on the other is the cat beginning to kill the rat; on one side is the rat, and on the reverse side is the rat gnawing the rope, etc.

Step Two: Introduce Print
George Shannon has two delightful books for beginning reading instruction, *Lizard's Song* and *Dance Away*.[3] Both have repeated parts which we highlight on the chalkboard and in the pocket chart. Children need to see print come to life from the end of a piece of chalk as well as seeing the same print on word cards and sentence strips.

Dance Away begins as follows:

Rabbit loved to dance.
He danced in the morning. He danced at noon.
He danced at night with the stars and the moon.
Every time he danced he smiled a big smile.
Everywhere he danced he sang his dancing song:
    left two three kick
    right two three kick
    left skip right skip
    turn around . . .

The song text is unpunctuated and we reproduce it as it is in the book, putting each word on a separate card in the pocket chart. We read the story orally from the beginning with dramatic emphasis, and each time

3. George Shannon, *Lizard's Song* (New York: Greenwillow, 1981); *Dance Away* (New York: Greenwillow, 1982).

we come to the refrain, "left two three kick," we point to the words and have the class chant. Rabbit sings this song completely nine times and two additional times with slight modification. In addition to the singing, we practice the dancing itself as we sing. When we have finished, the most common request is, "Read it again, please!" By the end of one session with twenty-plus chantings, most children have committed the dance text to memory. The teacher tracks by pointing to the words in the dance text as it is chanted by the children, and the children are invited to take turns pointing while the class chants. This tracking is necessary in developing the sense of a printed word, an essential understanding in learning to read. Many children have no idea what a printed word is, and until they do they have no success in learning to read. We discuss this issue again later when we describe teaching songs and poetry.

In *Lizard's Song*, lizard sings his song twenty-nine times:

> Zoli zoli zoli—zoli zoli zoli
> Rock is my home—rock is my home
> Zoli zoli zoli—zoli zoli zoli . . .

We make word cards or sentence strips or both. We read the story orally, pointing to the words when they recur, and the children chant. The children take turns with the pointing. Later the cards and strips go into the language center, along with several copies of the book, for children to retell and recreate the story. The children practice by putting the word cards in sequence, or by matching the word cards to the sentence strips if the first activity is too difficult. Many children will need lots of practice tracking before they are ready for this activity. This activity leads into step three.

Step Three: Children Match Word to Word

This is nothing more than having two sets of cards of familiar text. The children match by placing like cards on top of each other, or by building the repeated parts in the pocket chart. George Shannon's *Lizard's Song* lends itself to this practice. The teacher builds the first "Zoli zoli zoli," and the pupils build the next three. The teacher builds the first "Rock is my home," and the children build the second.

The Little Red Hen is available in several versions. The repeated chorus is written on the chalkboard or on strips placed in the pocket chart (fig. 5).

Each time the chorus is read, the teacher points to the words, and the pupils chant. The whole refrain is put on individual word cards, and the children match the words by placing the individual cards on top of the phrase cards. Or the teacher creates the first line with word cards, and the children build the second and third underneath.

To practice the story further we create patterned questions. The

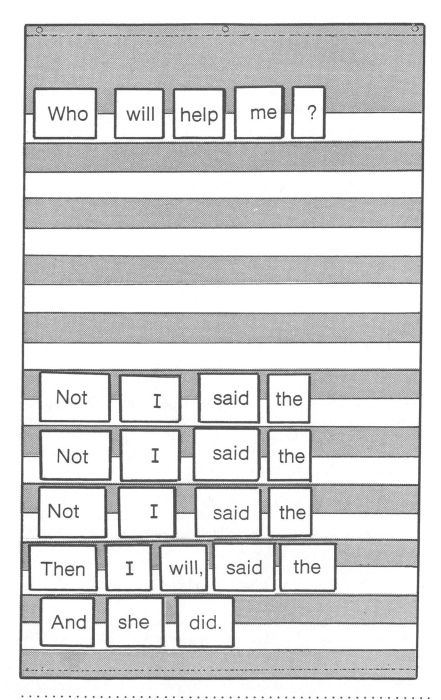

FIGURE 5. The Little Red Hen *in the pocket chart*

little red hen does all the chores. She sweeps the floor, washes the clothes, irons the clothes, washes the dishes, cooks the meals, etc. We make picture cards of each activity and put in the pocket chart the sentence "'Who will help me _____?' said the Little Red Hen" (see fig. 6). We put the picture of the dishes in the blank space, and the children read the question and the chorus:

> "Who will help me wash the dishes?"
> said the Little Red Hen.
> "Not I," said the dog . . . [etc.]

We change the picture to one of mowing the lawn, and everyone reads:

> "Who will help me mow the lawn?"
> said the Little Red Hen.
> "Not I," [etc.]

We have on cards the phrases "wash the dishes," "sweep the floor," etc., and next we use these rather than the pictures, or we use the pictures and distribute the phrase cards to the pupils, who match the print to the picture after we have read each part. This activity leads into step four.

Step Four: Children Match Words to Pictures

In Pat Hutchins's book *Rosie's Walk*,[4] Rosie the hen walks "across the yard," "around the pond," "over the haystack," "past the mill," etc. On separate cards we have pictures to represent "across the yard," "around the pond," etc. The children sequence the pictures, putting one card in each line of the pocket chart (see fig. 7). We put each phrase on a sentence strip, and then we tell the children that one of the phrases we will show them says "around the pond." One at a time, we hold up the phrase cards and ask the children to raise their hands when they see the card that says "around the pond." We ask them to tell us how they are sure, and we push them to apply phonics, eliciting such responses as:

> *Around* should end with a *d.*
> *Around* should have an *r* near the beginning.
> *Pond* should start with a *p,* have a *d* at the end.
> etc.

Before showing any cards we sometimes ask children to predict what letter should be at the beginning or end of each word. This application of phonics is vital in getting children to anticipate print. The pocket chart is filled with phrases to complete the story (see fig. 8). This matching is done many times directed by the teacher, and many more

---

4. Pat Hutchins, *Rosie's Walk* (New York: Macmillan, 1968).

FIGURE 6. The Little Red Hen's questions

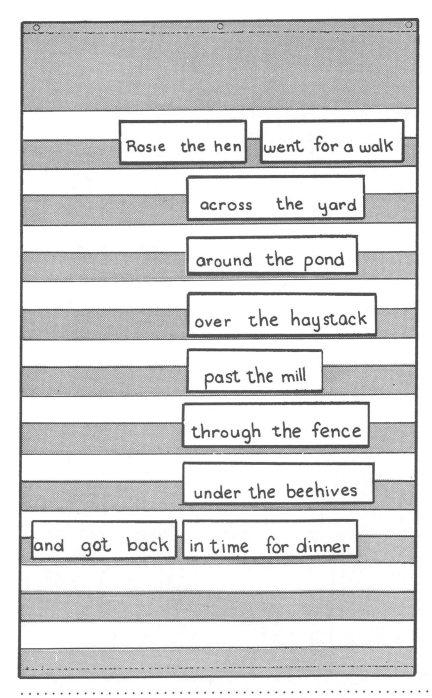

FIGURE 7. **Rosie's Walk:** *uncompleted pocket chart*

FIGURE 8. Rosie's Walk: *completed pocket chart*

times by the children individually and in small groups as they practice with the story.

Step Five: Children Match Pictures to Words
This is similar to step four but just a bit more complex. The words for *Rosie's Walk* are displayed in the pocket chart. Individual children are given a picture card to match to the words. Later the children are asked to recreate the story in the pocket chart using just the word cards. This leads into step six.

Step Six: Children Rebuild the Entire Story
We teach *The Happy Egg* by Ruth Krauss[5] from the "big book" version. We put the story on phrase cards and distribute them, one card per child, distributing the cards somewhat according to the difficulty of the card and the ability of the child. We ask who has the beginning of the story. Since most of the class have the story memorized, they tend to say the beginning aloud, and the child who has it merely has to recognize the words. We build the whole story in the pocket chart many times. The whole class participates in reading orally the part that has been built in the pocket chart to aid in getting the next phrase, and the class reads the whole story completely when it is finished.

Additional Books for Beginning Reading

The following are books which may be used to teach the previous six steps. With some we have fairly complete descriptions; with others we have merely listed the title and author and indicated by its placement the kind of book it is.

Brown Bear, Brown Bear, What Do You See? by Bill Martin, Jr.,[6] is perhaps the most universally used book in kindergarten and first grade in the United States. The pictures remind the children which animal comes next, if they have forgotten; the interlocking structure of the text lets the child know exactly what comes on the next page before the page is turned; and the repetitive pattern assures the child that he or she is correct.

> Brown bear, brown bear,
> what do you see?
> I see a red bird looking at me.

5. Ruth Krauss, *The Happy Egg* (New York: Scholastic, 1977).
6. Bill Martin, Jr., *Brown Bear* (New York: Holt, 1970).

Red bird, red bird,
what do you see?
I see a yellow duck looking at me . . . .

We work from lots of the old tales. Most have repeated parts which can be used in step 2–type exercises. Once heard, these tales are easily remembered. They have strong emotional appeal satisfying basic needs within children, thus making their repetition intellectually satisfying. They have structural repetitions that make word learning through rehearsal fairly simple.

For example, Paul Galdone's version of the *Three Little Pigs* states on the second page:

> The first little pig met a man
> with a bundle of straw,
> and he said to him:
> "Please, man, give me that straw
> to build me a house."[7]

On the third page is the sentence

> So the man did,
> and the little pig
> built his house with it.

We put both into the pocket chart on word cards; we change the words as indicated below in boldface type as the second pig begins to build his house.

> The **second** little pig met a man
> with a bundle of **sticks,**
> and said:
> "Please, man, give me **those sticks**
> to build me a house."

Followed on the next page with

> So the man did,
> and the little pig built
> his house **with them.**

Several pages later, after a repeated lot of huffing and puffing, we begin the house building of the third pig. The huffing and puffing refrain, of course, is also put into the chart for chanting as the story is read.

The story is predictable in many ways internally, not just because it has been heard. "The first" predicts that there will be "the second," and "the second" predicts "the third." "The third" might predict a fourth

---

7. Paul Galdone, *The Three Little Pigs* (Boston: Houghton/Clarion, 1970).

except that we have been told there would be no fourth by the first sentence of the story, "Once upon a time there was an old sow with three little pigs."

We present books like *The Three Little Pigs* in the pocket chart, in "big book" format, on word and phrase cards, and through creative drama, to help the children internalize the meanings and thereby learn the words in print.

We use Robert Kraus's *Whose Mouse Are You?*,[8] a delightful question-and-answer story in the form of a poem. Its choice of words is so exact that it seems impossible to change a single word without violating expectation. Jose Aruego's illustrations complement the text perfectly, making reading rehearsals possible for every child.

> Whose mouse are you?
> Nobody's mouse.
> Where is your mother?
> Inside the cat.
> Where is your father?
> Caught in a trap.

The logic of the questions and the emotion of an orphan's despair engulf the children. The resolution is equally satisfying:

> What will you do?
> Shake my mother out of the cat.
> Free my father from the trap.

We record the text on sentence strips, using one color of ink for the questions and a second color for the answers. We read it as a two-part drama, one group reading the questions and the second reading the responses. We pass out the question cards, one to each child, and the answer cards to other children. The children must find their partners. Then all recreate the text in sequence in the pocket chart. The cards become a learning-center activity in which one child or three or four recreate the text, take the parts, and read.

Mirra Ginsburg's *Where Does the Sun Go at Night?*[9] is a delightful fantasy in question-and-answer form that kindergarten and first-grade children enjoy.

Equally satisfying to children are the Spot books by Eric Hill. Reading these several times as "big books" usually enables children to rehearse them almost perfectly. In *Where's Spot*,[10] Spot's mother goes on a search to find Spot to call him to dinner. On page after page she asks,

---

8. Robert Kraus, *Whose Mouse Are You?* (New York: Macmillan, 1970).
9. Mirra Ginsburg, *Where Does the Sun Go at Night?* (New York: Greenwillow, 1981).
10. Eric Hill, *Where's Spot?* (New York: Putnam, 1980).

Is he behind the door?
Is he inside the clock?
Is he in the piano? . . .

Each object flips open with some animal other than Spot. A bear behind the door responds, "No." A snake inside the clock responds, "No." A hippo and its companion tick bird in the piano both respond "No." Spot is finally found and eats his dinner as mother says, "Good boy, Spot!"

Several matchings are available with *Where's Spot.* We use the questions on phrase cards and match them with pictures of the objects ("Is he behind the door?" matches with a picture of the door.) We use the same questions to match with the picture of the animal found "behind the door" or "inside the clock."

Mirra Ginsburg's *The Chick and the Duckling*[11] is another instant reader, a book that is learned completely enough in a single reading to permit rehearsal—although children are never satisfied with one reading. The duckling acts, and the chick imitates.

A Duckling came out of the shell.
"I am out!" he said.
"Me too," said the Chick.
"I am taking a walk," said the Duckling.
"Me too," said the Chick.

When the duckling goes for a swim, the chick plunges to the bottom, to be rescued by the duckling, who then says:

"I am going for another swim," said the Duckling.
"Not me," said the Chick.

The teacher reads the duckling part and the pupils respond as the chick. The teacher puts the text on sentence strips, reads the duckling part, and then challenges the children to read that part. As a class they are usually able to do this, and the teacher merely responds as the chick.

The book lends itself to creative drama, with half the class being the duckling and half the chick. We work in pairs for the rescue scene, and the dialog is memorized without the children being conscious of the memorization. The Aruego illustrations complement the text, so that no child fails in rehearsing the book, and the text is so predictable that there is little error in the rehearsal as the words are learned.

This book lends itself to sentence strip presentation in the pocket chart, and it is a simple, comprehensible way of introducing children to

---

11. Mirra Ginsburg, *The Chick and the Duckling* (New York: Macmillan, 1972).

quotation marks. We print the dialog in one color and the "said the Chick" or "said the Duckling" in another. We read the whole story and then we read it as dialog.

We use lots of counting books—books that count up and books that count down. The written numbers are anticipated and quickly learned visually. Usually some other structure aids the child's memory as well as the illustrations. Pat Hutchins's *1 Hunter*[12] is one of the simplest. She uses printed numerals for number words, and a portion of each illustration depicts part of the animal that is coming on the next page. The child has the number and the animal name fully in mind before turning the page to see the illustration and the text. "1 hunter" shows one hunter with a gun stalking through the forest with two elephants partially hidden behind the trees. We turn the page and "2 elephants" shows the two elephants fully watching the hunter walk among trees and the twelve legs of three giraffes. We turn the page and "3 giraffes" watch the hunter as he proceeds past four something. The hunter never sees any animals until he turns, sees them all and flees with a final text countdown of the 10 parrots, 9 snakes, 8 monkeys, etc. The story makes a marvelous mural, with each child contributing one or two animals. Styrofoam printing makes the illustrating very simple. The book lends itself to simple matching of numerical phrase to picture, and the dust jacket of the book provides small pictures that are easily mounted on cards for individual or small-group practice in the pocket chart.

Maurice Sendak's *Seven Little Monsters*[13] counts up and uses rhyme:

Seven monsters in a row, see the seven monsters go!
One goes up
Two go down
Three come creeping into town. . . .

This builds easily into the pocket chart with just pictures or with a combination of words and pictures. It becomes a "big book" easily: the pictures can be mounted and the print underneath each picture enlarged.

Robert Kraus's *Good Night Little One*[14] uses rhyme augmented by the whimsy of N. M. Bodecker's illustrations:

Good Night Little One   Day Is Done
Good Night Little Two   Peek A Boo, etc.

Each page is accompanied by a large numeral. The story lends itself to parody as teacher and older children create varying rhyming phrases:

12. Pat Hutchins, *1 Hunter* (New York: Macmillan, 1982).
13. Maurice Sendak, *Seven Little Monsters* (New York: Harper, 1975).
14. Robert Kraus, *Good Night Little One* (New York: Dutton/Springfield, 1972).

Good Night Little One   Have some fun
                                      Cinnamon bun
                                      There goes the sun
                                      No time to run

Molly Bang has a delightful going-to-bed countdown in *Ten, Nine, Eight,*[15] and John Becker's *Seven Little Rabbits*[16] is a complex countdown.

Tasha Tudor has done a counting-to-twenty book that uses rhyme and both numerals and spelled numbers. *1 Is One*[17] has a rhyme scheme between each two succeeding numbers:

1 is one duckling swimming in a dish
2 is two sisters making a wish . . .

11 is eleven girls dancing in a ring
12 is twelve baby birds learning how to sing . . .

The matching of numeral and printed number is an intuitive result of chanting and working with this book. Card pairs, one with the numeral and one with the spelled number, are a natural matching activity for younger children; with older children the book lends itself to writing parody.

Some books lend themselves to short phrase reading in which the phrases are a more poetic and natural response than complete sentences would be. In Robert Kalan's *Rain,*[18] the simple text can be read after only a few hearings because the illustrations identify the needed words, which are set boldly on the illustrations.

Blue sky
Yellow sun
White clouds
Grey clouds
No sun
Grey sky
Rain
Rain on the green grass
Rain on the black road
Rain on the red car. . . .

The text *Rain on the green grass* is color coded, being printed in green; *Rain on the black road* is printed in black; *Rain on the red car* is printed in red, etc.

15. Molly Bang, *Ten, Nine, Eight* (New York: Greenwillow, 1983).
16. John Becker, *Seven Little Rabbits* (New York: Walker, 1982).
17. Tasha Tudor, *1 Is One* (Chicago: Rand McNally, 1956).
18. Robert Kalan, *Rain* (New York: Greenwillow, 1978).

We make phrase strips duplicating the text, purposely not color coding them, and we create a picture card for each page of the book. Children can now create the whole story from memory using the pictures or the words, and they do all sorts of mixing and matching of the picture cards and the phrase cards.

The matching of pictures and phrases is a most important step. It is an application of phonics, and one of the first that children are able to do. They know that one of the cards says "white clouds." To sort this from all the others, including "grey clouds," requires close attention to the phonetic expectations of what the words should look like. The purpose of this activity is not to learn any of the particular words, although some children seem to learn every word that is used. It is to get children to work meaningfully with words; as a result every child seems to learn at least a few of the words for the day or week. Eventually, as children progress from directed attention to spelling and phonetic anticipation, as they write every day, and as words repeatedly reappear in different books, songs, and poems, some of the words do get into each child's memory bank.

Children move from this sort of work to creating their own rain books, adding their own ideas of where rain may fall:

> Rain on the school roof.
> Rain on the swing set.
> Rain on the playground.
> Rain on the teacher's car. . . .

Each idea is fully illustrated, and a self-authored book is created in which each child in the class has written a page. The children do the writing if they are able; the teacher takes dictation for those not able to write. The pages are duplicated, a title page listing each child as author and illustrator is created, a cover is designed, and each child gets an individual copy of the book. We make simple class books this way from lots of books. They are favorites of children during sustained silent reading periods.

Pamela Allen has written and illustrated *Who Sank the Boat?*[19] It has marvelously large print so that it can be used as a "big book" with small groups, and the illustrations are large enough to be viewable at a distance. It has repetition that requires the child to remember some fairly sophisticated language. After a short beginning, which introduces five friends, a cow, a donkey, a sheep, a pig, and a mouse, comes the question:

> Do you know who sank the boat?
> Was it the cow

19. Pamela Allen, *Who Sank the Boat?* (New York: Coward-McCann, 1982).

who almost fell in
when she tilted the boat
and made such a din?

Apprehension now should function to produce the answer, although perhaps not the exact words the first time the question is asked:

No, it wasn't the cow
who almost fell in.

Do you know who sank the boat?
Was it the donkey
who balanced her weight?
who yelled,
"I'll get in at the bow before it's too late."

The answer is now completely predictable if you have apprehended the pattern:

No, it wasn't the donkey
who balanced her weight.
Do you know who sank the boat?

The donkey does get into the bow, the cow does tilt the boat, so that *bow* and *tilt* potentially may be learned in at least one context made explicitly meaningful through the illustrations.

Anticipation of single words is developed through *At Mary Bloom's*, written and illustrated by Aliki.[20] The text reads:

My mouse just had babies!
I'll go tell Mary Bloom.
But if I do, I know what will happen.
Her door bell will ring
and the baby will cry
the dogs will bark
. . . So I'll call.
At Mary Bloom's
the telephone _____
the baby _____
the dogs _____

The children suddenly need to create past tense for the verbs, which they readily do, although not always the standard form. "The skunk shook" frequently becomes "the skunk shaked" requiring teacher intervention. Sometimes, the result is that the children say "shook," but often several children say "shook" and the rest say "shaked" until the story has been presented several times.

20. Aliki, *At Mary Bloom's* (New York: Greenwillow, 1976).

Later in the story all the past tenses need to be turned back to the present. This transformation is handled easily in the pocket chart by building the story with word cards, having *cry* on one side of the card and *cried* on the other, *bark* on one side of a card and *barked* on the other, *shake* on one side and *shook* on the other.

Aliki uses both printed words and rebuses to reprise the story so that the book is one that children can read and reread instantly with almost perfect memory of the words.

Our book *One Pig, Two Pigs*[21] uses illustrations to enable children to rehearse and read the text phrases. The phrases can be put on sentence strips and the pictures mounted for working in the pocket chart (see fig. 9).

> One pig on the table,
> Two pigs under the table.
>
> One pig in the car,
> Two pigs under the car. . . .

The children may write a parody illustrating their versions, with the teacher taking dictation if necessary.

Going for a Walk, by Beatrice Schenk de Regniers,[22] has a repeated pattern in which three words change with each repetition. The repeated part is as follows:

> She sees a _____.
> The little girl says Hi!
> The _____ says _____.
> The little girl walks on.

To tell this story we prepare picture cards and word cards. For example, the first animal the little girl meets is a cow. For this we have a picture of a cow on one card and the words *cow* and *moo* on cards. The teacher places the picture in the first blank and reads the next three lines. The other cards are either passed out or placed randomly at the bottom of the pocket chart (see fig. 10). After we have read the page, the pupils locate the two missing cards and place them in the proper space (see fig. 11). This requires an application of phonics as described in step five. We go to the next animal, the rooster, and complete the four-line pattern as we did for *the cow.* Children can work with this set of cards independently once the story has been presented.

We use our own *This Is the House That Bjorn Built,*[23] starting at the

---

21. Robert McCracken and Marlene McCracken, *One Pig, Two Pigs* (San Rafael, Calif.: Leswing Pr., 1973; Winnipeg, Manitoba: Peguis, 1986).

22. Beatrice Schenk de Regniers, *Going for a Walk* (New York: Harper, 1961).

23. Robert McCracken and Marlene McCracken, *This Is the House That Bjorn Built* (San Rafael, Calif.: Leswing Pr., 1983; Winnipeg, Manitoba: Peguis, 1986).

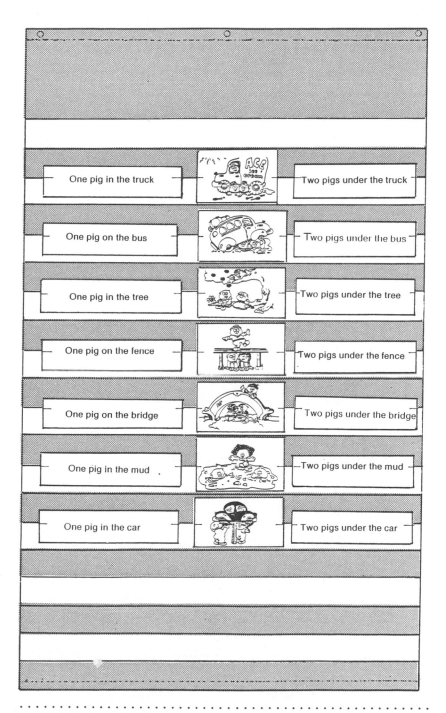

FIGURE 9. **One Pig, Two Pigs** *in the pocket chart*

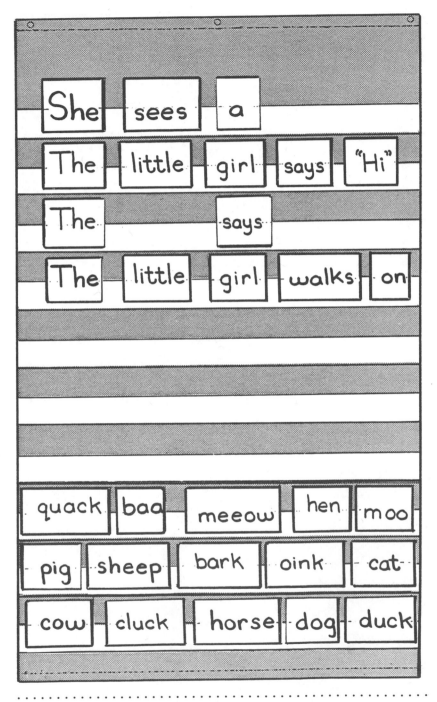

FIGURE 10. Going for a Walk: *uncompleted pocket chart*

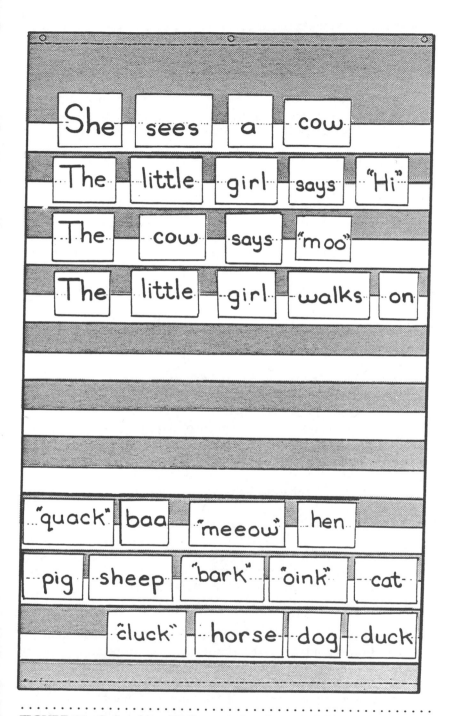

FIGURE 11. Going for a Walk: *completed pocket chart*

bottom of the pocket chart so that we can read the repeated parts downward as the story accumulates. We can build this with pictures as we did with *The Old Woman and Her Pig*, but we wish to describe the teaching of the book using words only. For efficiency we work with sentence strips with part of the story on either side of each strip so that we can tell the story easily by merely adding one strip and turning over one strip with each added action. For example we prepare the strips as follows:

Side One	Side Two
This is the house that Bjorn built.	that held the house that Bjorn built.
This is the tree with the nearby jail	that lived in the tree with the nearby jail.
This is the squirrel with the bushy tail	that barked at the squirrel with the bushy tail
This is the dog with the big soup bone	that petted the dog with the big soup bone.
This is the girl with the ice cream cone	that carried the girl with the ice cream cone.

We put card one in the bottom of the pocket chart and read:

CARD ONE: This is the house that Bjorn built.

We add card two and turn over card one to read:

CARD TWO: This is the tree with the nearby jail
CARD ONE: that held the house that Bjorn built.

We add card three and turn over card two to read:

CARD THREE: This is the squirrel with the bushy tail
CARD TWO: that lived in the tree with the nearby jail
CARD ONE: that held the house that Bjorn built.

We add card four and turn over card three to read:

CARD FOUR: This is the dog with the big soup bone
CARD THREE: that barked at the squirrel with the bushy tail
CARD TWO: that lived in the tree with the nearby jail
CARD ONE: that held the house that Bjorn built.

The ability to recognize the individual cards may seem beyond the children. However, it is not if they know the chant or poem or song by memory. Then the use of phonics is complex but not impossible, and working together, sharing insights into why a card can say what it is expected to say or why it can't be the right card, creates a powerful learning environment. Children have long attention spans and virtually unlimited ability when they work together to solve mysteries about language. What children are asked to do must be possible based on what they already know; it need not be simple. Many tasks that we traditionally give children to do to master skills are boring because there is so little to be learned from the exercise. Mastery of a visual form (word recognition) is a tenuous notion. As we learn to read we make fewer and fewer errors in word recognition, but we still make errors on some of the simplest words. I catch myself occasionally saying *a* for *the* or vice versa when reading orally; I suspect that I err more frequently than I know, because I probably do not notice the errors most of the time. I simply see what I think should be there. This is the reason that proofreading is a peculiarly difficult skill to master and why the proofreading of one's own work is exceedingly difficult.

So far, the books we have described are fairly simple and not overly long. There are a great number of more sophisticated books that are appropriate for beginning readers in grades two to four or even higher. Part of the art of teaching is being able to judge when a book is sophisticated enough to challenge without frustration. Some children will work happily with materials that are not particularly challenging and seem to be working productively, but they are not learning as much as they should or could. The following books are ones we have found to provide a challenge for older children who are still at a beginning reading stage.

Alexander and the Horrible, Terrible, No-Good, Very Bad Day by Judith Viorst.[24] The title of this book allows us to have children predict its content. We do this in either of two ways: (1) We tell the children that Alexander is five, in kindergarten, and that he has two older brothers. Now we brainstorm to predict what could happen to make his day horrible. (2) We may merely ask the children to recall things which make their days horrible. We put the phrase *horrible, terrible, no-good, very bad day* on the chalkboard or in the pocket chart and read the whole story orally, with the children joining in each time the phrase is used.

Following the oral reading we brainstorm for the things that actually made Alexander's day horrible. We classify the responses in three columns according to the time sequence of morning, afternoon, and night. We challenge the children to discover our classification rule. Almost always we get total recall of events from a class. We record the responses in a consistent manner so that they may be chanted in the following sentence:

> Alexander had a terrible, horrible, no-good, very bad day
> when _____.

24. Judith Viorst, *Alexander and the Horrible, Terrible, No-Good, Very Bad Day* (New York: Atheneum, 1972).

We chant all the responses in that frame; sometimes we repeat the chanting the next day. We put each response on a phrase card and use these to drill those children who need the help. We use the cards to have the children sequence the story and then to recall it as exactly as they can. We use the cards for classification, having the children sort the events according to some rule. We use the rules discovered to add to our own horrible events so that we can write a class book of tragedies. We suggest that not all days are horrible, and we create a parody such as *The Marvelous, Wonderful, Just Right, Very-Good Day* from which to write another class book. We rarely use *Alexander* below grade two and prefer grade three and above because the book is not viewed as funny by children until they are two or more years above the kindergarten level of Alexander.

By teaching *Alexander* we have made the text accessible to remedial reading pupils, and we have given all children a book they can reread several times to develop their word-recognition skills. We find that some children would rather read a mature book such as this thirty or forty times than simpler books which seem to be at more appropriate reading levels.

George Shannon's *The Piney Woods Peddler*[25] has repeated parts and repeated patterns in which a few words change as the peddler walks and meets different people. He sings a song:

> With a wing wang waddle
> And a great big straddle
> And a Jack-fair-faddle
> It's a long way from home.

We put this on sentence strips and place it in the pocket chart.

The peddler has an opening pitch he makes to each new person he meets:

> Trade you my horse
> Trade you my ring
> For a shiny silver dollar
> I'll trade anything.

We put this refrain on sentence strips and put it in the pocket chart. The thing to be traded changes as the story progresses, and so word cards are placed on top of the word *horse*. The peddler's song and opening pitch are repeated many times in the story, and the class reads them orally each time the story is told.

We make word cards for each character in the story and three cards for each item they will trade. We make the trading frame as follows:

---

25. George Shannon, *The Piney Woods Peddler* (New York: Greenwillow, 1981).

_____ said, "Got no shiny silver
dollar, but we can trade just the
same—my _____ for your _____."
So the Piney Woods peddler swapped his
_____ for the _____
and off he went.

We distribute the word cards to the pupils prior to reading the story orally. The text that we read predicts which cards will go into the blanks, and the pupils must make the prediction to know if their card is to fit. We reteach this story, and many of the stories, many times. This repetition gets the story into the remedial pupils so that they can work with the text meaningfully.

The Judge by Harve and Margot Zemach[26] builds easily down the pocket chart, or it can be written on the chalkboard for its repeated parts. One by one, five prisoners are called before the judge by the court announcer with a rhyming couplet and sentenced by the judge with a rhyming couplet. Each prisoner tells the judge about the monster, saying:

A horrible thing is coming this way,
Creeping closer day by day.
> Its eyes are scary.
> Its tail is hairy.

Each prisoner repeats the preceding prisoner's report and adds a couplet to describe the monster. The teacher reads the story with dramatic flair, and the pupils read together the parts in the pocket chart as they are built downward. Children enjoy writing couplets of their own devising to add to the description of the monster.

The Fat Cat by Jack Kent[27] builds down the chart similarly once the cat begins to eat. We read the introduction to the story orally without pictures to the point where the old woman returns and asks, "Now what has happened to the gruel?" As the cat replies, "I ate the gruel," we put a picture of a spoon in the third line of the pocket chart, and as the cat says, "And I ate the pot, too," we put a picture of a pot in the fourth line. We have prepared pictures of all the characters in the book, and as the cat says to each one, "And now I am going to eat YOU," we place the picture in the next line.

Skohottentot and each succeeding character says to the cat, "What have you been eating my little cat? You are so fat." We have this printed on cards and we put this at the top of the chart so that the children can join in with the first reading and thereafter (see fig. 12).

26. Harve and Margot Zemach, *The Judge* (New York: Farrar, 1969).
27. Jack Kent, *The Fat Cat* (New York: Parents Magazine Pr., 1971).

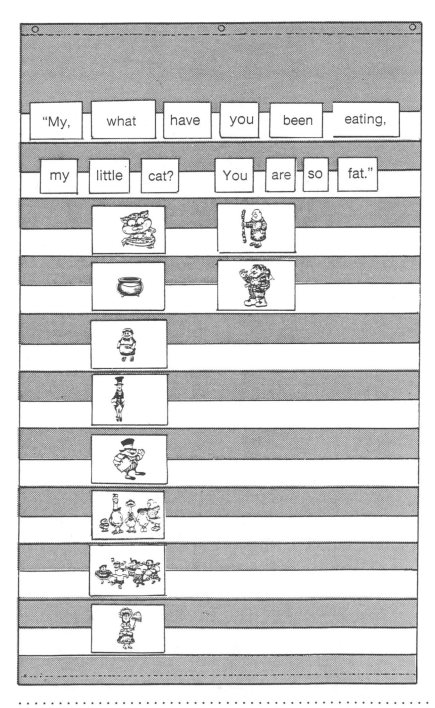

FIGURE 12. The Fat Cat *in the pocket chart*

At the story's end, we remove each character as it exits from the cat's stomach and then pass out the cards, one per child, to be replaced in the pocket chart. When the children have worked with this story in rebus form, we pass out sentence strips that say "old woman," "Skohottentot," "Skolinkenlot," "five birds in a flock," etc., and rebuild the story using the words. The pupils can work to match words and picture.

Usually we try to read whole stories without interruption, representing the whole story visually for the presentation. However, some stories do not lend themselves to total representation. With *Bringing the Rains to Kapiti Plan* by Verna Aardema[28] we read the introduction that precedes the accumulating parts orally before we begin the pocket chart presentation. This is a complex African folktale that we would not use until grade two at the earliest.

All in the Morning Early, by Sorche Nic Leodhas,[29] is a Scottish tale that builds the same way.

Antonio Frasconi's *The Snow and the Sun*[30] is an Argentinian version of *The Old Woman and Her Pig.* With minor adaptation in technique it builds up the chart and is easily changed downward by the children following either text or pictures.

28. Verna Aardema, *Bringing the Rains to Kapiti Plain* (New York: Dial Pr., 1981).
29. Sorche Nic Leodhas, *All in the Morning Early* (New York: Holt, 1963).
30. Antonia Frasconi, *The Snow and the Sun* (New York: Harcourt, 1961).

5

Spelling

We once talked to a successful writer who said he had had a terrible spelling problem. "Before I learned to spell easily I often forgot what I planned to say as I concentrated on how to spell."

Children learning to write face this same problem. Writing requires that children have something to say, that they have the vocabulary to say it, and that they know what structures they will use. However, children still cannot write with ease if they are unable to spell almost automatically. Further, some children have the same difficulty in learning penmanship. They have to think so directly about the handwriting and how to shape the letters that they forget what they are trying to say. This same forgetfulness happens to adults learning to type as they search for the keys. A child beginning to write need not spell perfectly, just as a writer using a typewriter need not be a polished typist, but a child has to spell easily enough that attention can be directed to the message. However, spelling must be good enough that the message can be read. We do not mean to denigrate correct spelling or the learning of it. Correct spelling occurs after a child understands how to spell. Knowing how to spell enables the child to soon spell so easily that the mind can concentrate on the message, not upon the form.

Spelling, a Developmental Skill

Teachers and parents are likely to view spelling somewhat differently than other skill-learning tasks. A child's efforts in learning to talk are often incorrect or terribly inarticulate, yet as parents we converse as well as possible, ignoring the mistakes or errors. As adults, we enjoy and chuckle inwardly at a child's counting, "one, two, three, four, six, seven, ten," or at the countless stumbles and falls a child makes as he learns to walk. There is no expectation of perfection or errorless attempts. Teachers teach addition facts and expect the child to practice the addition facts, correcting mistakes as the child learns to add. The teacher teaches addition and then assigns addition for practice. He or she would never consider assigning percentage, ratio, fractions, or even subtraction problems for practice. The child is expected to practice what has been taught. Spelling raises different specters, different expectations. When children write, they are frequently expected to spell perfectly. A grade-one child's head may be full of messages to record, but to record these messages may require grade-three, or five, or even adult spelling ability. The child is expected to spell these words correctly even with virtually no instruction in spelling. This expectation is akin to assigning grade-one children percentage or ratio problems after teaching simple summing of the numbers from zero to five. If we have taught just the beginnings of spelling, a child can make reasonable attempts in spelling words, but there will be lots of errors—errors that are necessary as part of learning to spell. Correcting all the errors will not help; it will help no more than standing a fallen child erect will prevent a fall in the next attempt to walk. Spelling is learned developmentally, just as arithmetic and walking are. A first step in spelling is understanding the alphabetic nature of the code used in written English.

Teaching Spelling

Many children explore the mysteries of the writing system without formal instruction and deduce both correctly and incorrectly about the nature of spelling. Our purpose in teaching spelling is to develop each child's ability to spell easily before incorrect spellings become habituated and need to be unlearned. We need to teach about the spelling system in such a way that all children discover how the alphabet works so that they can begin practicing writing with attention focused upon messages, not upon the perfect spelling of words.

Learning to spell should be a fairly simple task. It usually is if the child does not become overly concerned and confused when beginning. Some children in trying to learn to spell become confused and decide that spelling is hard, too difficult to learn, with the result that they never attend to spelling in order to learn it. Learning how to spell is not learning the correct spelling of individual words. Most adults have intuited how spelling works and have generalized, correctly spelling thousands of words they have never been taught. They are able to do this because they generalized correctly and because they understood the spelling system. They know that the letters of the alphabet represent the sounds of speech within a spoken word, and that the general direction for spelling is left to right. With this understanding, both the regular and the seemingly irregular spellings of English can make sense, and phonics can be used sensibly in learning how to spell.

This concept of alphabetic writing is the foundation of spelling, just as understanding addition and subtraction are foundations for learning percentage, fractions, and other mathematics. Math is more than memorizing the number facts of addition, subtraction, multiplication, and division. Spelling is more than the memorization of the correct spellings of thousands of words.

Requisites for Learning How to Spell

The beginning of this chapter has been a long preamble to stating that understanding spelling requires two insights. (1) Children must intuit what a word is. (2) They must understand two concepts about alphabetic writing: [*a*] spoken sounds are represented by letters, and [*b*] the letters are written in the sequence in which the sounds are uttered. Children must realize that when you say a sound you write a letter and that you write the letters in a left-to-right sequence.

Sources of Confusion in Learning to Spell

Before explicating further, let us examine why some children may be confused in learning how to spell. Some of these ideas are very old, having been promulgated many years ago by those who wanted to reform English spelling. George Bernard Shaw was a noted advocate of spelling reform in the early 1900s, and Sir James Pitman was a strong advocate in the 1950s and 1960s, supporting the augmented Roman alphabet, or I.T.A. (Initial Teaching Alphabet). Both Shaw and Pitman suggested that reading problems were caused by irregular English spellings, noting that English has only twenty-three useful letters to represent more than forty English phonemes and that *q, c,* and *x* duplicate sounds already represented. They contended that children have difficulty cracking the code because some letters alone and several letters in combinations represent more than one phoneme. They were correct. Many children become terribly confused by what they see as inconsistencies. For example, why spell *fez* and *pheasant* differently at the beginning when both begin with /f/? Why use *c* to spell /k/ in *come* and /s/ in *city*? And why spell /um/ in *come* with *ome* and then use *ome* to spell *ohm* as in *home* or *Rome*. (Someone may wish to state the rule that *c* followed by *i* represents /s/, but this is not the reason. The reasons for strange spellings are numerous, not the least of which is merely variation and change in spoken dialect since spelling became standardized. The inventors of English spelling did not sit and ordain that sometimes the syllable /sit/ should be spelled *sit* as in *sit, cit* as in *city, site* as in *opposite,* and also represent /zit/ in words such as *transit.*)

Even more perversely, the long vowel sound of /a/ may be represented by

ay as in *say* but not in *aye*
ey as in *they* but not in *eye*
eigh as in *neighbor* but not in *height*
e as in *cafe* but not in *safe*
et as in *Chevrolet* but not in *let*
ai as in *rain* but not in *plaid*
ei as in *rein* but not in *reinstate*
a-e as in *came* but not in *camel*
a as in *rabies* but not in *rabid*

It is possible to explain these spellings, but not to a six-year-old trying to learn to read. The lack of consistent correspondence between sound and symbol obscures the basic alphabetic relationship, making it impossible for some children to intuit the understanding necessary to learn how to spell.

We talk in a constant flow of syllables, articulating only as clearly as necessary to be understood. *We .. do .. not .. talk .. in .. words. Wetalkin-phrases. Wetalkindifferentphrases. Wetalkinsentences. However, we write in words.* We write:

"How-r-yuh?" as "How are you?"
"Jeet?" as "Did you eat?"
"I wanna," as "I want to."
"I hafta-go," as "I have to go."

Writing requires that children know what a written word is, a very difficult concept. It is learned intuitively by working with print that is meaningful. It cannot be learned by definition. Children can learn to write before or while they are learning what a printed word is, however. Most children begin writing without leaving spaces between words, as any grade-one teacher will affirm. It may be that writing is one of the best ways to learn what a printed word is.

We have very rarely met a child who had difficulty learning to respond orally to the printed numerals from 0 to 9. With printed numerals a single symbol represents a single word or idea. A one-to-one relationship exists (one word = one symbol, or one word = one idea) for all ten symbols. The one-to-one relationship does not hold for spelling. If we were to invent a writing system we would do as Pitman did. We would provide 44 or 45 symbols so that we could assign one to each phoneme consistently. This would greatly simplify understanding the code and make the alphabetic principle discernible. The World Literacy program begun by Frank Laubach used this notion in creating written languages. However, even with simplification, learning about words is harder than learning about numerals. In speech it is phoneme combinations that convey meanings, and frequently these combinations involve several words. For example, "Once upon a time" represents one idea, but each of the words is used in many other combinations to represent other ideas.

We have met children who in attempting to solve the code have assigned wrong understandings to the letters of print. They have tried to solve "Once upon a time" by assuming that each letter represents a word. They assigned:

o to once
n to upon
c to a (uh)
e to time

When this failed to make sense, some tried assigning:

o to one
n to /s/
c to (uh)
e to pon
u to u (uh)
p to time

When this also failed to work, some struggled and changed to some other system that finally made enough sense that they could learn. Some children, however, have persisted with incorrect assumptions, never succeeding but never changing their assumptions. The frustrations of repeated failure and their confusion made the cracking of the code seem so impossible that they concluded that reading and writing could not be learned; they ceased trying to make sense of the code and remained illiterate.

Teaching a child about phonics and spelling is not a matter of choosing the correct system. It is a matter of focusing upon the understanding necessary for any system to be grasped and thereby making the system accessible to learning. The first understanding that children must intuit is that *print is a form of language*. The second understanding is that *print has some arbitrary characteristics*. The two most important arbitrary characteristics are the concept of a printed word (letters surrounded by a blank space of sorts) and the use of letters to represent phonemes. This last notion is difficult to discern with traditional spelling because we have so many letters that are used to represent sounds that have changed or been dropped from the oral language. (The /hw/ is gone from *which* in most speech; the /er/ is gone from *interesting*, which has shifted to "in-tres-ting" in most speech.) We have borrowed many foreign words in print but have pronounced them in an English manner. We have had to use some letters to represent more than one sound, since we have too few letters in the Roman alphabet to represent the sounds of English.

Children listening to a conversation use the social context and the differences among words to derive meanings. They discriminate with virtually no error between such imperatives as:

"Please pass me the sugar" and "please pass me the salt"
"Go to bed" and "go to bat."

They have no difficulty with any of the following in a context that makes sense:

Bring me the bit.
Bring me the bat.
Bring me the bait.
Bring me the butter.
Bring me the boat.
Bring me the beet.
Bring me the beater.
Bring me the heater.

It is difficult to think of any real context in which any two of these requests are equally likely. Children discriminate readily from speech in which there is very little phoneme difference; in the examples given, there is roughly one phoneme difference in ten phonemes. It is meaning that makes this such a simple activity, just as meaning is central to working with print. To listen, children attend to differences. To spell, however, children must attend to likenesses within speech. They must know that *bring* is part of every request on the "bring list," and they must discern that it is also part of the sentence "What did mother bring?" Additionally, they must discern that /b/ and /r/ in the combination /br/ are in *bring, brought, bride,* and *bright*. Spelling focuses attention on the form of the language, not the meaning.

We have checked children by using pictures to test their discrimination of speech commands, such as "Point to the picture of the _____" (bat, bait, boat, etc.). Virtually all kindergarten children who could identify the pictures responded correctly. With the same children we found very few aware of *point, to, the, picture, of,* and *the* as repeated words. We found very few who seemed aware of the /b/ or /t/

likenesses. Without these understandings it is not surprising that some have difficulty in learning to read and write.

We commonly assume that children in learning phonics must learn to hear likenesses and differences. This may be the ultimate result, but we know that children learning to write pay attention to their mouths. We find that many children are more likely to feel the likenesses when saying *bring, bride, brought,* or *boat, bat, bit* than they are to hear the likenesses. We find that some children watch the teacher's mouth, just as the child with a hearing loss watches to see the message. We find that many children have greater difficulty when listening to a recording than when watching a teacher say words. For these reasons we focus upon the feeling of sounds, asking children, "What did you say?" rather than, "What did you hear?" when they are learning to spell.

Written English is not completely alphabetic; there are common spellings or printings which do not represent all of the phonemes with letters. Our numeral and number system in print is not phonetic, nor is +, −, &, and $. Yet all are easily read. No one worries that they are not phonetically written. All abbreviations represent only a few phonemes of the spoken word. *Mr., Mrs., Dr., St.,* and *Ave.* are all read easily. Children learn abbreviations with little difficulty even though they are not solvable through phonics. Almost all abbreviations are fraught with meaning, which may account for their being learned easily. The consonant /y/ is not represented in the standard spelling of *few, beauty, continue,* etc. Without the /y/ *few* would be *foo, beauty* would be *booty,* and *continue* would be *continoo.* None of these exceptions is important once the child has sensed the basic notion of an alphabetic code. The child comes to realize that the code is a good guide for checking one's predictions as to what word an author is using, that there are lots of extra letters, an occasional lack of letters, and some erratic letters that represent many sounds. Children accommodate these irregularities automatically if they have not been taught to expect total regularity, and if they are taught so that they can learn how spelling works.

We have explicated our preferences for teaching phonics and spelling in *Spelling through Phonics*[1] and partially in *Reading, Writing and Language,*[2] so we will present this subject only briefly here. We do lots of work with the pocket chart, using word cards and pictures to represent poems, songs, and nursery rhymes to develop a sense of what a printed word is. We do lots of chart and chalkboard work to develop beginning writing through frame sentences. This again develops a sense of the

1. Marlene J. McCracken and Robert A. McCracken, *Spelling through Phonics* (Winnipeg, Manitoba: Peguis, 1982, 1985).

2. Marlene J. McCracken and Robert A. McCracken, *Reading, Writing, and Language* (Winnipeg, Manitoba: Peguis, 1979).

printed word. We teach the phonics of spelling in small groups, and we demand lots of writing and correct spelling insofar as it has been learned.

We begin formal spelling by teaching four things together. We teach the letter *m*, for example, by teaching:

1.   The name of the letter
2.   The sound the letter represents
3.   The feel of the letter within the mouth
4.   The way the letter is written.

We do this with small chalkboards or by sitting around a chalkboard table. We tell the children that they will learn about a letter. We have the children say the letter name and make the letter sound. We have the children feel what they do with their mouths in making the sound, noting that the sound is part of the name for those letters for which this is true. For example, to teach /m/, we have the children say the letter name, *em*, asking what they do with their mouths to get them to associate the sound with the feeling. We show the children how to write the letter, and they print the letter on their chalkboards. We start teaching with consonants because vowels are so erratic in their representations, and because vowels cannot be felt and discriminated within the mouth. We have children divide their chalkboards into four equal rectangles and have them put two short lines in each. (See fig. 13.)

We teach the children which box is number one, which is number two, number three, and number four. Now we dictate four words that either begin or end with /m/. We say *marvelous*. The children repeat the word and indicate the /m/ by printing *m* on the first line in box number one. We say *mutt*, and children indicate the /m/ by printing *m* on the first line in box number two. We say *gram*, and the children indicate the /m/ by printing *m* on the second line in box number three. We say *mustard*, and the children complete box number four. As we dictate we say each word only once, modeling the correct pronunciation, then require each child to say each word as often as necessary to discriminate the sounds. (Of course we repeat a word if the children mispronounce it.) To write and spell, children must be able to encode their own speech, a very different process than encoding the speech of someone else. We erase our *m*'s and dictate another four words. As the children write, we nag to get the letters in the right places and to get the penmanship to a good standard. The dictation lesson is short, rarely exceeding five minutes for any group. On subsequent days, the lesson is repeated two or three times, always using different words. The purpose is to learn how to spell, not how to spell certain words through memorization. On the

FIGURE 13. Child with chalkboard marked and ready for dictation

third or fourth day a second letter is introduced, *t*, perhaps. Dictation proceeds as before except that when *met* or *movement* is dictated, the child is required to write both *m* and *t* in the proper sequence. Once a letter has been taught it is demanded thereafter until it is finally learned.

All children have a penmanship book in which they practice making both capital and lower-case forms of the letters. They write two lines of lower-case letters and two of capitals. They copy two to five words that they find around the room which contain the letter of the day. They each draw twenty to forty small pictures representing words that they know orally in which there is an *m* or the letter of the day. Most of the pictures will have the /m/ in initial position.

We teach six consonants before we teach any vowels, and then we introduce short /a/, followed by another six consonants. The abler children frequently generalize by this time and write quite freely, spelling phonetically, sequentially, indicating that they have grasped the basic notion of letters representing sounds in a left-to-right print sequence. Others will be struggling, only beginning to understand the notion after they have had several error-loaded lessons, because they need to be taught ten or fifteen letters before they can generalize.

As soon as a vowel has been introduced we help the children to spell whole words or syllables. In one sense there is no such thing as an easy word or a hard word. All words are either single syllables or combinations of syllables. Most syllables are combinations of two or three sounds. There are words that are hard to spell in that they have unusual patterns or unexpected letter combinations to spell a common syllable. Thus *beaux* is harder than *bow*, which in turn is harder than the proper name *Bo* or the last syllable in *hobo*. If we have taught the letters *m, s, f, b, t, a* and *ing* and the child has learned them, we expect the correct spelling of *mat, stab, fast, Sam, bat, bats,* but we also expect *fascinating* to be spelled *fasnating*—although the *n* may be expecting too much since it has not been taught specifically. Most children who have learned those six letters and *ing* will generalize enough to use the *n* from learning *ing* and from the writing that has been done from frame sentences.

The sequence of subsequent teaching varies depending upon the writing and spellings that the children are using in their writing. We may teach:

1. Another short vowel, usually /o/
2. *S* as a plural, whether pronounced /s/ or /z/
3. Another six consonants (a total of eighteen have now been taught)
4. The remainder of the consonants
5. *Y* as representing long /e/ on the end of words, so that children can spell words such as *sandy, badly, candy, rusty, lumpy,* etc.
6. *Ing* as an ending because children need *ing* to write freely.

In doing these last dictations we have begun the final step in teaching spelling, the teaching of patterns. Learning to spell becomes a lifelong process. For example, this book is being written with both an American and Canadian readership in mind. How should we spell *favor* (favour), *practice* (practice and practise), *check* (cheque as a bank draft)? Spelling is not an absolute. *Travelled* and *traveled, develope* and *develop,* etc., are all acceptable by some authority.

Two final notes: Some highly used words are nonphonetic in their expectation. If children are to write daily and spell these words as they anticipate, they will misspell them so often that they will commit misspellings to memory. We call these words *doozers;* we post five of these prominently within the room and insist that childen spell them correctly. We begin doozers in December in grade one and in September in all other grades. *They* is our most common doozer because some children spell *they* as *thay* and maintain this wrong spelling seemingly forever. *Does, because, is, the, come,* and *have* are doozers. Once a doozer seems to have been learned, we replace it with another.

After December in grade one and after day one in all other grades, we refuse to spell for pupils who ask how to spell. The children must spell as well as they are able to in order to practice the phonics they are being taught. The teaching is useless without the practice, the application. It is through practice that children internalize all the *rules* they need for independent word recognition. The rules are intuited rather than directly stated. Intuited rules rarely are applied incorrectly; rules taught to children frequently are applied with poor results. Eve Merriam's poem "Why I Did Not Reign" sums the thought:

> I longed to win the spelling bee
> And remembered the rule
> I had learned in school:
>
> "I before E,
> Except after C."
>
> Friend, believe me,
> No one was going to deceive me.
>
> Fiercely I practiced, the scepter I'd wield,
> All others their shields in the field would yield!
>
> Alas, before my very eyes
> A weird neighbor in a beige veil
> Feigning great height and weighty size
> Seized the reins and ran off with the prize.
>
> Now I no longer deign to remember the rule.
> Neither
> Any other either.[3]

We teach children to spell syllabically and demand that they practice as they write. Their writing tells what they have mastered, what they are learning, and what they apparently need to be taught in their small dictation groups. We correct what we have taught by nagging children as they write. When a child has attempted a word beyond his or her ability, we nag to get the spelling as correct as possible, so that just any spelling is not accepted, even through what we accept is not correct. Spelling becomes the phonics-teaching program, with daily writing the natural way to practice phonics.

---

3. Eve Merriam, "Why I Do Not Reign," in *It Doesn't Always Have to Rhyme* (New York: Atheneum, 1964), pp. 68–69.

6

Beginning Writing

We have mentioned that writing requires four things: something to say, the vocabulary to say it, the structures with which to write, and the ability to spell. At first these four are so overwhelming that writing seems an impossible task for young children. However, it proves not to be. Children seemingly are eager to explore writing, even more than reading. We can capitalize on this natural interest and make first writing highly successful if we teach children how to write.

Frame Sentences

Most children come to school filled with enough information to have something to write about. If not, we teach; even when children come filled with ideas we still teach content as one of the main functions of school. We have already described many forms of brainstorming. We brainstorm as one way of getting content for children to write. On day one of grade one we ask all the children to respond to one question. For example, "What can you see?" As each child responds the teacher records each response on the chalkboard, using a frame sentence as a structure plus a hastily drawn picture. A frame sentence is a normal response to a question. "What can you see?" yields the frame response "I can see a(n) _____." On day one we use each child's name instead of *I*, so that the chalkboard becomes filled with responses such

Frank can see a

Carmen can see a　　　.

Lucy can see a　　　.

Bob can see　　　.

Thomas can see an　　　.

Mary can see a　　　.

Charlene can see a　　　.

We record one response for every child. We read orally and we reread the responses several times chorally. The use of the children's names seems to increase their ability to remember what each child saw. We have the children participate by spelling their names if they can. This is an informal test. We also have the children participate by chorally spelling *can* and *see* several times as the teacher writes. These oral activities keep all the pupils active and learning. This is a long session which theoretically is beyond the attention limits of most children. However, we have taught this lesson more than 200 times within the first week of school and find that almost all children attend fully.

The next step is to get each child's sentence recorded on an individual sentence strip. We have prepared sentence strips on which we have already written *can see* with space to the left and right:

can see a

Each child reads his or her own response, and the class echoes each child's reading. We ask each child to spell his or her own name as we quickly write the name on a *can see a* sentence strip and complete the response with a hastily drawn picture. Each child reads the whole sentence as the completed strip comes from the teacher; the teacher points to each word as the child reads it aloud. Those who have no sense of what a word is will need close attention in a few minutes.

Now we are ready for individual chalkboard work. Each child copies his or her own name and *can see a* or *an* and draws a picture. The teacher watches carefully to help those few children who may need help.

Each child now indicates with fingers where to cut the sentence strip in order to cut it into words. The teacher distributes scissors to those who know where to cut and helps those few who are uncertain. Every child cuts the sentence strip into words and recreates it several times, reading aloud and shuffling the cards after each try. This is a noisy, productive period. The children choose buddies and swap cards, recreating each other's sentences with whatever help the buddy has to give.

Next they recreate their own sentences and copy them as full sentences on their chalkboards. If they are successful, and most are, they take their cards and with paper and pencil write their sentence one or more times by copying under each word. They usually want to write the sentence several times. For writing we use unlined paper that has been folded into fours or sixes so that the children have a space within which to write. We use unlined paper now because many children cannot yet control the size or position of their letters well enough to succeed on lined paper. This ends lesson one.

The next day the teacher asks the same question but substitutes *I* for each child's name, filling the chalkboard with pictured responses and having the children read and reread the responses chorally. They practice writing *I, can, see, a,* and *an* on their chalkboards. Each child writes a favorite response in a full sentence on the chalkboard, using a drawing for the final word, then erases, and does a second one. The children are taught how to fold their paper into six or four, and each writes a page full of responses. A few children may require a sentence strip that says "I can see a _____" to place on their paper to copy under. The teacher may obviate by having "I can see a" on the top of a few photocopied sheets for those who may need the help. We find the photocopying is rarely needed if the chalkboard work has been done.

The next day we merely repeat the question, with less time spent in the brainstorming of answers. We provide a set of picture-card nouns and several sentence strips saying "I can see a _____." The children place a picture in the space and read the sentence, change the picture and read another sentence. We may change the question to "What can you see at the supermarket?" so that all the responses become store items with the children putting in only pictures that belong. We may change to "What can you hear?" or "What can you do?" These simple writings are merely a quick way of getting children into successful writing. Other parts of the program are taught concurrently and begin to impinge upon the child's brain. Overemphasis upon frame-sentence writing will lead to stilted, repetitive, uncreative writing; we use it sparingly with some children and carefully with all.

We extend our questioning to force children to think beyond the mundane and obvious. We ask children what they can do. They respond *see, walk, eat, hop, run*, etc. We take one or more of the responses to work with for a day or two. For example, we may develop the following with *run*, doing one each day:

I can run to	I can run after
I can run through	I can run around
I can run over	I can run with
I can run on	I can run under

We develop meaning for the various prepositions, and we develop the various meanings of *run*. We substitute an animal for I—*dog*, for example—and redevelop the list.

A dog can run to
A dog can run through
A dog can run over

Frame sentences are productive for a short time. The amount of instruction needed before writing is not great. By using primarily ideas that children bring with them, the teacher need not spend a lot of time developing ideas to use within the frames. The teacher is freed for other kinds of teaching that need to be done at the beginning of grade one, and the children learn to work independently for fairly long periods so that the teacher can take small groups for spelling dictation, math instruction, and other skill lessons.

We develop frame answers from questions about stories that children know well. For example, children pretend that they are Red Riding Hood and write in response to the wolf's question, "What do you have in your basket, Red Riding Hood?" They respond using the frame "I have _____ in my basket." We teach some children about commas in a series. In November we got responses such as:

I have blueberries, strawberries, and oranges in my basket.
I have Aspergum, Alka-Seltzer, and Rolaids in my basket.
I have pizza, chewing gum, and cake in my basket.

The answers came as a result of brainstorming and the recording of answers on the chalkboard as an idea bank from which anyone may choose. Most of the answers were simple sentences such as:

I have gum in my basket.
I have milk in my basket.

When children first do frame-sentence work or any writing, they tend to copy words from the chalkboard so that there is very little misspelling. The spelling of some words, such as *the* and *I*, get learned from repeated use within a frame. As children gain control over how to spell, they tend not to waste time looking for words on the chalkboard in order to spell, and they misspell phonetically. *Apple* becomes *apl, pizza* becomes *petsa* or *petesa,* and *cake* becomes *cak* or *kak*.

We develop frame stories by asking questions and recording the answers:

What pet do you have?
How big is it? What shape is it? What color is it?
What can it do?
What can't it do?
How do you feel about your pet?

Combined, the frame answers create a frame story:

I have a _____.
It is _____, _____.
and _____.
It can _____.
It can't _____.
_____.

From this we get such writing as:

I have a frog.
It is green, bumpy, and as big as an orange.
It can hop and jump high.
It sits and stares.
It can swim under water.
It can't ride a bike.
It is the best pet I have ever had.

We do not demand that the responses fit precisely in the frame. In fact, we encourage the opposite so that children write naturally as they develop the ability.

Frame sentence and frame story writing are used sparingly, even though they are simple to do and even though children love to do them. One of the problems with frames is that some children clutch to them. \

We avoid this by very early moving into freer writing patterns based upon song, poetry, and favorite stories. We want children to use and imitate the finest patterns that we can provide. Children's books, songs, and poetry provide such patterns. Frame sentences demonstrate the basic structures of English, but they are not the finest models. If we use the finest of models, many children will grasp and develop an exquisite sense of literate prose, and all will learn the basic sentence structures.

Building a Noun Word Bank

We build a list of nouns to develop a concept. We classify the list to develop the concept, and we use the list for reading and writing activities. For example, we ask, "What is part of fall?" and use the responses. Our example reflects British Columbia and the Pacific Northwest.

We print *What is part of fall?* on the chalkboard and allow time for the children to read it silently.

A child says, "Fog."

We print *fog* on the chalkboard. We point to *fog* and then to each word needed to answer the question fully—"Fog is part of fall"—as we have the children read orally. We read in a normal cadence as we track.

A child says, "School."

We print *school* next to *fog,* starting a second column. Again we point, and the children chant, "School is part of fall."

A third child says, "Blackberries."

We print *blackberries* in a third column, and point to lead the children in reading chorally, "Blackberries is part of fall." If the children say *is,* we ask if *is* sounds right. If the children say *are,* we point to *is* and ask them what we need to write on the chalkboard. We write *are* under *is* and tell the children that sometimes they will need to use *is* and sometimes *are.* They are to decide as they give responses, and everyone is expected to chant the right one.

A child responds, "Rain."

We write *rain* under *fog* as we classify the answers according to some rule. Again the children chant as we track. We take four or five more responses, classifying the responses according to our rule. Responses that do not fit into a category are used to head a new column.

A child says, "Recess."

We ask, "Where does it go?" If the child says that it goes under *school,* we put it under *school* because this fits our rule. If a guess is wrong, we say, "It doesn't fit my rule," and allow another guess or two before we put it under *school.* Thereafter, we challenge children to tell us where their responses go. We do not ask them why. We allow the classification to be a mystery that everyone gets a chance to solve as additional words are added.

After an hour or so of oral work, a first- or second-grade word bank may look as follows (this will require at least two chalkboards):

What	is	part	of	fall?
A				
An	are			

fog	school	blackberries	witches
rain	books	apples	masks
frost	pencils	pears	ghosts
mist	erasers	peaches	skeletons
coolness	teachers	plums	jack-o-lantern
ice	recess	blueberries	goblins
snow	desks	grapes	pirates
puddles	homework	jam making	fireworks
dead leaves	sack lunches	jelly making	werewolves
icicles		canning	Dracula
bare branches			warlocks
wind			candy
slush			trick-or-treat
gray skies			phantoms
clouds			haunted houses
short days			Frankenstein
long nights			poltergeist
			parties
			bonfires
			the bogeyman
			black cats
			brooms
			bats
			spiders
			vampires

Other columns

Thanksgiving	corn	coats	geese
turkey	squash	boots	robins
cranberries	cabbage	toques	ducks
pie	onions	sweaters	swallows
holidays	pumpkins	raincoat*	swans
grandma	tomatoes	mittens	hummingbirds
goodies	carrots	earmuffs	bears
ham	potatoes	wool socks	badgers
candies		galoshes	beavers

(Continued)

cookies	hats	groundhogs
	umbrella*	frogs
		toads
		foxes
		chipmunks
		squirrels

*To chant *raincoat* we need *A* and to chant *umbrella* we need *An* at the beginning of the sentence so that it sounds right. We print *A* and *An* under *What* and tell the children to use the word they need.

These lists begin the developing of the concept of fall. Each column can be added to, and additional columns may be started. We teach about fall by observing, by reading to children, and by providing other learning experiences. We almost always get a listing of the new TV shows and fall sports. We get a listing of fall chores, particularly gardening activities in the rural areas.

Class secretaries print all the words on individual word cards. We make two sets. One set is hung on the wall, affixed to strips of masking tape. We usually hang the lists in categories. The second set is for hands-on use.

Classifying

We give twenty to thirty of the fall word cards to a group of three or four children. We group the children so that each group has a child who is likely to know most of the words. We tell the children to sort the words into two classifications. We try to guess the rule after the words have been sorted. This is a productive activity but one that takes time, particularly as children are beginning the activity. Each day the children are regrouped and given a different set of thirty cards. We allow about ten minutes each day. If a group finishes in less, we guess their rule and ask them to think of another classification. We can ascertain the children's breadth and depth of understanding from their classifications.

After about a week of free sorting, we ask the children to sort according to our rule. We place the rule in the pocket chart in the form of an incomplete sentence:

_____ is alive.

We tell the children to sort their cards into two groups of subjects, those that are alive and those that are not.

Simple Reading and Writing from Classifications

While the children sort, we prepare the pocket chart for reading and writing activities, as follows:

_____ is alive.
_____ is alive.
_____ is alive.
_____ is alive.
_____ is alive.
But a _____ is not alive.

Each group fits their word cards in the appropriate spaces, and the class reads the sentences while the teacher or one of the group tracks the words. When each group has had a turn, all the word cards are removed, leaving the empty sentence strips. The children can now write individual versions, placing their favorite answers in each space. Grade-one children are able to write six sentences this way early in the year. Other contrasts that could be used with the fall noun bank are:

Things you can wear; things you can't.
Things you can eat; things you can't.
Things you like to eat; things you don't. (This is a very personal list.)
Halloween things; not Halloween things.
Things that grow; things that don't.
Things you can hear; things you can't.
Things that frighten you; things that don't.
Things that are orange; things that aren't.
Things you have at home; things you don't.

We make beginning reading books for first grade from our noun word bank. We choose something that we know the children know a lot about, such as *spiders,* and we ask, "What do you know about spiders?" We take answers so that they complete the frame sentence "Spiders _____." We print the responses as we get them on three-by-ten-inch cards. Typical responses would be:

are black
have eight legs
make webs
eat flies
spin silk

We print *Spiders* on a card for a cover and we staple the cards into a book. We show the children how to read the book by saying "Spiders" as we turn each page to read:

Spiders are black.
Spiders have eight legs.
Etc.

Writing Lists

Lists are perhaps the easiest structures for children to write. Lists can be very simple or quite sophisticated.

The Simplest List. The simplest list is a series of nouns:

Fall is apples,
            rain,
            bonfires,
            corn,
   and pumpkins.

We develop list writing in the pocket chart so that children may see the format. We use word cards and blank word cards as "word holders" to make it easy for children to follow the structure. (See fig. 14.) The children use the words from the word bank as they practice orally saying different lists many times before actually writing.

Making a Simple List Sophisticated. We vary the simple list in six different ways.

1. We add adjectives to our noun list with word holders in the appropriate places in the pocket chart:

Fall is _____ apples,
       _____ rain,
       _____ bonfires,
       _____ corn,
   and _____ pumpkins.

The children practice saying several versions—for example:

Fall is delicious apples,
      cold rain,
      brilliant bonfires,
      golden corn,
      and orange pumpkins.

(We may add two adjectives to each with older children.)

2. We add verbs to our nouns, practicing from the pocket chart:

Fall is apples _____,
      rain _____,
      bonfires _____,
      corn _____,
   and pumpkins _____.

The children chant, practicing several versions such as:

Fall is apples ripening,
      rain falling,

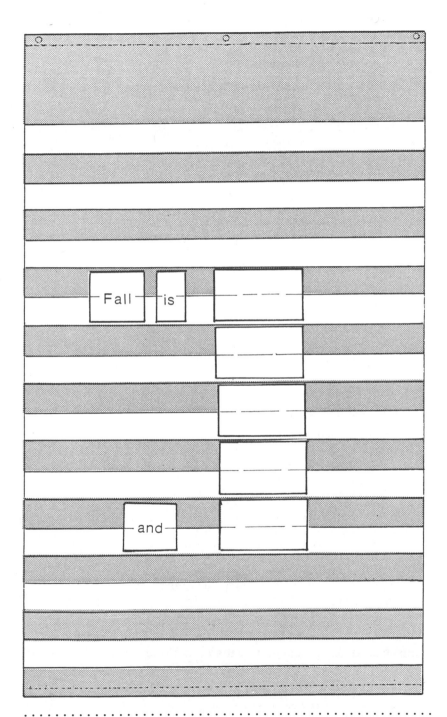

FIGURE 14. Pocket chart holding the structure for "Fall is"

bonfires blazing,
corn tasseling,
and pumpkins glowing.

3. We use both adjectives and verbs, chanting from the pocket chart:

Fall is _____ apples _____,
_____ rain _____,
_____ bonfires _____,
_____ corn _____,
and _____ pumpkins _____.

Fall is delicious apples ripening,
cold rain falling,
brilliant bonfires blazing,
golden corn tasseling,
and orange pumpkins glowing.

4. We add prepositional phrases to our nouns, modeling in the pocket chart:

Fall is apples _____,
rain _____,
bonfires _____,
corn _____,
and pumpkins _____.

Children chant, creating:

Fall is apples on the trees,
rain on the window pane,
bonfires in the gardens,
corn in the fields,
and pumpkins in the patch.

5. We combine all of these, preparing the pocket chart, and creating such oral chants as:

Fall is delicious apples ripening on the trees,
cold rain falling on the window pane,
brilliant bonfires blazing in the gardens,
golden corn tasseling in the fields,
and orange pumpkins growing in the patch.

6. We create countdowns. Countdowns are lists, either simple or sophisticated, using numerals or the days of the week as an additional structure. Two examples:

I knew it was fall because:
On Monday I saw one colored leaf.
On Tuesday I saw two ripe apples.

On Wednesday I saw three geese flying south.
On Thursday I saw four squirrels gathering nuts.
Etc.

One is the fog covering our morning.
Two are the nights becoming colder and longer.
Three are the apples getting redder and riper.
Four are the pumpkins waiting for Halloween.
Five are the colored leaves swirling to the ground.
Etc.

Frame Sentences and Patterns with the Noun Bank

1. We use frame sentences for children just beginning to write. We place one or two in the pocket chart and have the children practice orally, using the words from the noun bank. When they can say the sentences fluidly, we set them to writing. They are expected to write six sentences a day. The sentences may all follow one frame or some combination of two or more frames that have been introduced earlier and practiced orally. For example:

In the fall I can see _____.
In autumn I see _____.
There are many _____ in autumn.
The _____ tell me it's fall.

2. Commas in a series are a bit harder:

In the fall I can see _____, _____, and _____.
There are _____, _____, and _____ in the fall.
I like to play _____, _____, and _____ in the
fall when school starts.
My favorite autumn days are _____, _____, and
_____.

These may be simply nouns; for beginners nouns are sufficiently challenging. However, the frames will sound better when combined with adjectives, verbs, and prepositional phrases. The expectation should suit the abilities of the children.

3. We may work with participles and adjectives:

Fall is a leaf
Twisting, twirling, turning.
    Fall is chrysanthemums
    glowing, glistening, growing.
Fall is football
With *uniforms, stadiums,* and *cheering crowds.*
    Fall is Halloween
    With *goblins, ghosts,* and *witches*
    moaning, groaning, and screaming.

Creating an Idea Bank

We create idea banks by brainstorming with the children. The teacher does the recording. We write *witches* on the chalkboard with a blank line in front of it.

_____ witches

We ask the children, "What kind of witches do you know?"

As the children respond, we record each answer, and they chant the new word and ten or more words from the list. We try to get lots of words—the more the better. In grade one at the beginning of the year, and with English as a second language classes, we can work with as few as 20 words. In upper grades we have gotten more than 100. We need 40 or more to do classification activities. This takes lots of chalkboard space and lots of time. Getting the adjectives may be one day's lesson. We ask what witches do and elicit verbs. We ask where they do these things and get a long list of prepositional phrases. In grade three and above, we may ask when or why or how they do these things, getting as many as six lists of words and phrases. We use these lists to develop sentence sense, concepts about how written language works, concepts of the meanings, and as an idea bank for writing. We read to the children during this brainstorming time to add colorful language from authors who have written about witches. We have used Ian Serrailler's *Suppose You Met a Witch,*[1] reading such portions as:

> There's one I know, all willow-gnarled and whiskered head to toe. We drowned her at Ten Foot Bridge last June, I think—but I've seen her often since at twilight time under the willows by the river brink, skimming the wool-white meadow mist astride her broom o' beech.

From this we extract the words and phrases *willow-gnarled, whiskered, under the willows, by the river brink, skimming,* and *astride brooms o' beech.*

This results in an idea bank that looks in part as follows (except in grade one, there usually would be more words than are reproduced here):

terrible	**witches**	fly	by the haunted house
warty		scream	in the dark dark woods
wild		chant	near the drippy cave
scraggly		cast spells	under the rotting floor
scrawny		brew	by the mill
willow-gnarled		cook	in the school
whiskered		cackle	under the teacher's desk
dreadful		read	by the river brink

1. Ian Serrailler, *Suppose You Met a Witch* (Boston: Little, 1952, 1973).

beautiful	stumble	under the willows
fearsome	peer	astride a broom o' beech
ugly	watch	near the tombstone
bad	remember	through the sky
good	worry	through the gloom
insane	wobble	through the moonlight
fat	wonder	over the moon
skinny	wish	behind the school
enormous	dig	in the cemetery
wicked	bake	by the cauldron
hungry	hide	around the stewing pot
tiny	tremble	over the covered bridge

The words recorded must come from the pupils. It might seem that time would be saved by giving children the words, since we can predict many of the words they are likely to suggest. We have found that when we impose the words upon the pupils they are uninterested in working with them for extended periods of time. When we take the time to brainstorm, every child learns enough words to participate, and all children seem to maintain interest for a lengthy period of time.

Using the Idea Bank

The teacher has each word or phrase transcribed onto word cards or sentence strips, making two complete sets. Generally the cards are made by the pupils or by having upper-grade children come to grade one to make the cards. We use the cards in the pocket chart, creating various lists for chanting with no set order, and for children to work with. The other set is hung as a master list on masking tape where it can easily be seen.

We now do a great number of activities using the idea bank. We use it to practice word recognition, but more important, we develop concepts through classification of the words or ideas. We also work with sentence structure and the syntax of print. The following suggestions exemplify the types of activities we do using an idea bank.

1. *We chant the lists*—using enough language to make the chanting meaningful—i.e., we don't just chant words.

a) We use adjectives and chant:

terrible witches
warty witches
wild witches
scraggly witches

b) We use verbs and chant:

witches fly
witches scream
witches chant
witches cast spells

c) We use prepositional phrases and chant:

witches by the haunted house
witches in the dark, dark woods
witches near the dripping cave

2. *We create song parodies*, singing and writing.
a) We use "The Farmer in the Dell":

Witches by the mill,
Witches by the mill,
Flying, screaming, casting spells,
Witches by the mill.

or

Wild, warty witches
Wild, warty witches
Through the sky
Behind the school,
Wild, warty witches.

b) We create to the tune of "Are You Sleeping?":

Witches flying, witches flying,
Through the sky, through the sky.
Wobbling and trembling, wobbling and trembling,
On their brooms, on their brooms.

or

Warty witches, warty witches,
Cooking brew, cooking brew.
Casting spells and chanting,
Casting spells and chanting,
By the cauldron, by the cauldron.

c) We create to "Skip to My Loo":

Witches by the cauldron
Casting spells,
Witches by the cauldron
Casting spells,
Witches by the cauldron
Casting spells,
Halloween is coming.

Cackle, cackle
She'll get you.
Cackle, cackle
She'll get you.
Cackle, cackle
She'll get you.
If you go trick or treating!

We do all of this composing orally, with the teacher serving as secretary at the chalkboard or rearranging words in the pocket chart. We use these three songs because they have the repetition that makes the activity fairly easy to do and helps children still uncertain of print learn the words as visual forms. What we model and practice orally becomes a structure for writing for small-group or individual work.

3. *We develop sentence sense* through oral work with the idea bank.

a) The teacher points to words, creating a full sentence. The children follow, reading with their eyes. The teacher points a second time, and the children read orally together.

b) The teacher builds sentences in the pocket chart. The children read with their eyes and then chorally.

c) Pupils take the teacher's role.

d) The teacher works with the syntax of the language, helping children become aware of the sounds of English. Adjectives and nouns are placed randomly into the pocket chart. For example:

wild skinny witches
warty dreadful witches
tiny terrible witches
scrawny willow-gnarled witches
whiskered scraggly witches

The chart is read in unison, and the teacher asks, "Do all the phrases sound right?" We move the cards in the pocket chart in response to the pupils' comments. This is an informal test of sorts. Children who have heard enough spoken and written English will never tolerate "warty dreadful witches." This is not a matter of learning a rule but a matter of intuitively responding to preferred syntax. There is no need for the teacher to strive to create these examples. They occur regularly if we randomly place the words in the chart. We hope children will prefer "dreadful warty witches" to "warty dreadful witches," and "scraggly whiskered witches" to "whiskered scraggly witches."

4. *We work with the meaning of the language* by randomly adding verbs and prepositional phrases to the nouns and adjectives. For example:

Ugly witches watch near the tombstones.
Bad witches remember through the sky.
Wicked witches bake by the cauldron.
Tiny witches tremble over the covered bridge.

The teacher asks, "Do all the sentences make good sense?" With luck, some children will not like "Bad witches remember through the sky" or "Tiny witches tremble over the covered bridge." We look for better endings or add to the idea bank if necessary. We are working here with sentence sense, developing the most common sentence structures intuitively. Those children who do not respond easily to this work are telling us that they have not experienced standard syntax enough to have acquired this sensitivity. We find this a common characteristic of children learning English as a second language; they need to hear stories over and over, and they need to chant and sing with the total class so that these melodies become theirs.

5. *We work with sentence structure.* To groups of three or four pupils, we give eight adjectives, two nouns, four to six verbs, and four to eight prepositional phrases. (With grade one at the beginning of the year we give fewer cards.) We now have them create sentences following the models we have made in the pocket chart. We usually achieve this by asking a question or giving a direction that concerns meaning. "What can witches do?" or "Tell me something about witches that is true on Halloween." Children spread out their cards and create sentences. This is a writing activity that requires no penmanship, so that children get to practice making many sentences fairly quickly. The activity may be repeated on subsequent days, but the groups of children should change and the cards that any one group works with should also change. When children have a sentence that they like, we challenge them to use the same cards in a different order and still keep a good-sounding sentence. Often children can make two or three transformations. If we are working with four types of words as we do in grade three and above, several transformations are possible.

6. *In small groups we have children classify the cards.* We do this in two ways.

a) Children classify any way they wish.

b) We ask a question such as "Which of your words describe how a witch might move?" From the verb list, they would choose "fly, stumble, wobble" and any others from the extended list that fit. Note that to classify, the words must be recognized but the meanings must be used also, so that this sort of flash-card work deals with reading, not just word pronouncing.

c) As quick drill, we put any four words of the same type—i.e., adjectives, verbs, etc.—in the pocket chart. We ask, "How are the four words alike?" or "Which word doesn't fit?"

d) Other quick drills include such requests as:

Find a word that means the same as _____.
Find a word that means the opposite of _____.
Find a word that has two syllables.
Find a word that rhymes with _____.
Find a word that tells a size.
Find a word that sounds like _____ at the beginning.

7. *We work with verbs.* We work with shifts of time and number. We say, "This list tells what the witches did today. Tell me what the witches did yesterday." We now chant the verb list transformed into the past tense. We have pupils classify the words according to what happens to the written word in a shift to the past tense. Which words just add *ed*? Which words change their entire form (e.g., *bring-brought*)? Which words double a consonant or drop an *e*? We change *witches* to *A witch* and work with the verbs orally, chanting, "Witches fly but a witch flies. Witches brew but a witch brews."

8. *We discover rhyme.* We classify the verbs to find rhyming words. With forty or more verbs, there will be some rhymes. We will find that we can create simple rhymed poems. For example:

Old witches cry
Young witches fly.
Terrible witches moan
Dreadful witches groan.

We shift the rhyme into medial position and create such forms as:

Old crying witches,
Young flying witches.
Terrible moaning witches,
Dreadful groaning witches.

We shift the rhyme scheme to model other possibilities:

Crying witches,
Moaning witches,
Flying witches,
Groaning witches.

We work with internal rhyme as indicated above as well as with traditional rhyme at the end of the line. We do lots of oral practice, and children can write simple four-line rhyming poems.

9. *We do patterned writing,* using fairly long patterns. Some of these are story patterns and some are poetic patterns.

a) Our most-used pattern is Margaret Wise Brown's "Bugs."

> I like bugs.
> Black bugs,
> Green bugs,
> Bad bugs,
> Mean bugs,
> Any kind of bug,
> I like bugs.
>
> A bug on the sidewalk,
> A bug in the grass,
> A bug in a rug,
> A bug in a glass,
> I like bugs.
>
> Round bugs,
> Shiny bugs,
> Fat bugs,
> Buggy bugs,
> Big bugs,
> Lady bugs,
> I like bugs.[2]

We substitute *witches* for *bugs* and use our own adjectives, verbs, and prepositional phrases. Children very easily write their own witch poem.

> I like witches
> Warty witches
> Wild witches
> Weird witches
> Wonderful witches
> Any kind of witch
> I like witches.
>
> A witch in the haunted house
> A witch in the dark, dark woods
> A witch by the cauldron
> I like witches.

2. Margaret Wise Brown, "Bugs," in *The Fish with the Deep Sea Smile* (New York: Dutton, 1938), p. 74.

b) We use Mina Lewiton Simon's book, *Is Anyone Here?*[3] The first two pages of the book ask:

Is anyone here?
Is anyone here?
Where the sea
nibbles the land
of rock and sand?

Is anyone tall,
Is anyone small,
sunning,
or crawling
or plodding
or running?
Is anyone here?
Is anyone near?
No one is here!
No one
EXCEPT

We usually present this much of the poem in the pocket chart, asking the children to tell where the author is and to predict the next line.

We establish that no one is here except a witch and we work with our verbs from the idea bank. We change them into participle form to fit the following pattern:

No one is here!
No one
EXCEPT
a witch
_____, or _____, or _____
_____, or _____, or _____

We also note how the poet has chosen to say "seashore"—i.e., "where the sea nibbles the land of rock and sand." We use the prepositional phrases from our idea bank and we extend them to

where the ghostly shadows flit by the haunted house
where the grey mist rises from the dark, dark woods
where the bats swoop near the dripping cave

We get such responses as:

No one is here!
No one

3. Mina Lewiton Simon, *Is Anyone Here?* (New York: Atheneum, 1967).

EXCEPT
a witch
howling, or yowling, or scowling,
or ranting, or chanting, or incanting,
where the cauldron bubbles in the dark, dark mist.

c) We use the following poem, for which we have no name or author:

I'm listening
    for spring to come,
    for breezes to blow,
    for bees to hum,
    for brooks to flow,
    for birds to sing,
    and then I'll know
    it's spring.

In parody we get:

I'm waiting
    for Halloween to come,
    for goblins to scowl,
    for witches to howl,
    for cats to yowl,
    for ghosts to fly,
    for werewolves to cry,
    and then I'll know
    it's Halloween.

We make several shifts with the poem as the pattern. We can change listening to waiting, watching or hoping for, etc. We can change spring to any holiday, season, day of the week, month of the year, etc. This can become a pattern for writing throughout the year.

d) We present Margaret Wise Brown's *The Rabbit Skip:*

Hop Skip Jump
A rabbit won't fight.

Hop Skip Jump
A rabbit won't bite.

Hop Skip Jump
A rabbit runs light.

Hop Skip Jump
He's out of sight.[4]

4. Margaret Wise Brown, "The Rabbit Skip," in *Nibble, Nibble* (New York: William R. Scott, 1959).

The pattern is self-evident to most children, so the teacher moves to modeling. We need three verbs that go together in some way. This is easy if the children have been doing lots of classification work, sorting words into categories. The second line of each couplet rhymes and tells a story. We do not emphasize the rhyme. In fact we sometimes model without attempting rhyme purposely to establish that the rhythm is sufficient to maintain the structure. From witches we get such parodies as:

Watch Peer Stare
Witch plans her flight.

Watch Peer Stare
Witch flies into night.

Watch Peer Stare
Witch hides from sight.

Watch Peer Stare
To you tonight.

or

Cackle Chant Incant
Witch begins to brew.

Cackle Chant Incant
Witch stirs her stew.

Cackle Chant Incant
Witch adds some poison, too.

Cackle Chant Incant
Witch casts her spell on you.

e) We use whole books or parts of books as models for imitation. We use lots of books and stories that have been developed earlier as reading and chanting patterns.

We use Pat Hutchins's *Rosie's Walk*.[5] The text begins, "Rosie the hen went for a walk. . . . " (Prepositional phrases are used throughout the book to tell where Rosie went.) The book ends, "And got back home in time for dinner."

We take Wanda the Witch for a walk or a ride in the sky and get back in time to scare the children or to cast a spell.

---

5. Pat Hutchins, *Rosie's Walk* (New York: Macmillan, 1968).

Wanda the Witch went for a walk
Past the graveyard
Around the tombstone
Through the haunted house. . . .
And got home in time for the clock to
strike bong, bong, bong, bong, bong, bong,
bong, bong, bong, bong, bong, bong!

We use the beginning of George Shannon's *Dance Away* to create songs. *Dance Away* begins:

Rabbit loved to dance. He danced in the morning. He danced at noon. He danced at night with the stars and the moon. Everytime he danced, he smiled a big smile. Everywhere he danced he sang his dancing song:

left two three kick
right two three kick
left skip right skip
turn around. . . . [6]

We change rabbit to witch and decide what she might love to do, and we invent witch's song:

Witch loved to cackle. She cackled in the morning. She cackled at noon. She cackled at night with the stars and the moon. . . .

or

Witch loved to brew. . . .
Witch loved to fly. . . . etc.

Mary Ann Hoberman's *A House Is a House for Me* is a favorite book of children, and one that stimulates all sorts of unusual thoughts. It can be used as a structure for early writing, adapting itself to Halloween purposes as well as many others. It begins:

A hill is a house for an ant.
A hive is a house for a bee.
A hole is a house for a mole or a mouse
And a house is a house for me.
A web is a house for a spider.
A bird builds its nest in a tree. . . . [7]

Children create such ideas as the following about Halloween:

A black hat is a house for a witch's head.
A cauldron's a house for a brew.
A cave is a house for a cauldron.
A ghost is a house for a BOO!

6. George Shannon, *Dance Away* (New York: Greenwillow, 1982).
7. Mary Ann Hoberman, *A House Is a House for Me* (New York: Viking, 1978).

Writing from Lists

Although we have not said so, much of the writing that we have been describing has been the writing of lists. Lists are perhaps the easiest thing to write. There are no rules about writing lists except the implied concept that a list contains things that "go together." This rule organizes our thinking and writing. There are no punctuation marks required and no capital letters to worry about, although you can make a list using capital letters and punctuation. Much of poetry is lists, so we use lots of poetry that is in list form, or we imitate that part of a poem that is a list. Bette Killion's "Think of It"[8] uses a list within each stanza; "Bugs" is three lists put together; "A House Is a House for Me" is a rhymed list; each verse of "She'll Be Coming round the Mountain" is one item on a list; "Is Anyone Here?" incorporates lists within its body. All the writing that we did about witches originated from the lists, lists that were grammatically organized. We needed to subclassify each list to get the ideas better organized for writing.

Thus we need the word lists to help us write with ease. We hang the second set of words on the wall, using masking tape to make long lists. We merely affix each card on the sticky side of the masking tape and then hang it high in the room. The tape usually holds for the two to four weeks that the words are being used unless the air is exceedingly dry. This gives us a ready reference for all the words, while we still have the first set to sort, build, and work with.

Some stories are lists of a sort, and we have children use them as a basis for writing. Pat Hutchins's *Rosie's Walk* is a list of places where Rosie walked. We have already indicted how we can have children parody this. Jack Kent's *Fat Cat* was discussed for pocket-chart use. The beginning is delightfully uncluttered; and the ending with the woodchopper cutting open the cat is the obvious and perhaps the only satisfactory resolution for the story, but the middle can be changed or extended. The Fat Cat can eat a different array of people, so that we can rewrite the middle.

The Farmer and the Skunk go on a merry chase around the farm; there are lots of additional places they could go, so that the middle can easily be rewritten. We can do this kind of rewriting individually, or we may want to compose a class version where groups of children write sections, which are put together in a final stapled version for class use. Sometimes we create books for every child in the class with the Ditto machine. We always put in a title page with thanks to the original author and illustrator and put the pupils' names in as authors and illustrators.

The Zemachs' classic retelling of the old tale *The Judge* is one in which the middle can be extended. The Zemach version has five

8. Bette Killion, "Think of It" in *Poetry Place Anthology* (New York: Instructor Publications, 1983).

prisoners, each of whom adds a couplet to further describe the on-coming monster. We have added prisoners up to thirty-two in one extended version. To the teacher, this seemed too much, but the children reveled in the length.

Rewriting Stories

We have already indicated that children rewrite prose stories into song form. We have found that some stories interest children sufficiently that they have asked if they can write their own versions. The resulting stories range from mere condensations to inventions that bear little resemblance to the original except for an episode or recurring phrase. We mention this because we still continue to be surprised when children so willingly do this. The key, of course, is a powerful, well-loved story. It may be that the retelling eliminates all the problems that are faced when creating a story except for spelling, so that there is a sense of quick accomplishment.

One very successful rewriting evolved from a grade-three class's study of folktales as a structure, and in particular reading and comparing versions of *Little Red Riding Hood*. They located thirty-two versions of the story and then decided to individually write their own versions. Most were liberal interpretations adding such modern accoutrements as telephones and chewing gum. A typical grade-three version of *Little Red Riding Hood* is as follows:

> Once upon a time there was a sweet little girl named Little Red Riding Hood. One day her mother asked her to take some wine and cake to her grandmother. Her mother said, "Do not loiter on the way." "O.K., Mother," she said. So she went to the path in the woods. She was walking down the path picking flowers for her grandmother. And she got startled from the wicked old wolf. Then the wolf asked, "Where are you going, Red Riding Hood?"
>
> "Down to grandmother's house."
> "Where does she live?" asked the wolf.
> "Down on the other end of the forest."
> So the wolf ran to grandmother's house and knocked on the door. Grandmother said, "Come in."
> The wolf rushed into the house and swallowed grandmother whole. And then the wolf put on grandmother's clothes and got into bed. Red Riding Hood knocked on the door.
> The wolf said, "Come in."
> And Red Riding Hood said, "Grandmother, what big ears you got."
> "The better to hear you with, my dear."
> "What big eyes you got."
> "The better to see you with."

"What big hands you have."

"The better to hug you with."

"And grandmother, what big teeth you have."

"The better to eat you with, my dear," and the wolf jumped out of bed and ate her.

The woodsman came and heard the wolf snoring, so he went in and almost shot the wolf. "But maybe the old lady is inside," so he cut the wolf open and the old lady jumped out and Red Riding Hood ran to get some stones to put in the wolf. She put some in and when the wolf tried to run away he dropped over dead. The woodsman took the wolf skin home.

They lived happily ever after.

[Darron Drake]

A different Darren in grade one in April rewrote *Goldilocks* as follows. The spelling and punctuation are as he wrote it. This is excellent writing, but it is not unusual writing for some children in a class that has had spelling and writing instruction and practice since September.

One day my family went for a drive. Well we were gone a little girl named Goldilocks came. First she peeped through the window. Next she looked in the keyhole. Then she enterd through the window. First she tried my dad's telephone but it was too heavy. Then she tried my moms telephone but it was too soft. Then she tried my telephone. It was just right. Then she went and tried on some shoes. First she tried on my dad's shoes. They were too big. Then she tried on my mom's shoes. They were too small. Then she tried my shoes. They were just right. Then she went upstairs and tried my dad's bed. it was too big. Then when we came home and saw her she saw us and scamperd out of the house.

Joey's story is more typical of average achievement in its spelling.

One day we went to the park. Wen we were gone goldilocks came in our drive way. She went in the dore. and then she went in my sisterts room. and turned on the radeo. Then she went in my moms and dad's room. then she went in my room and turned on the radeo.and then she would watch tv in the living room.then she would make some bacon. then we came home and we saw goldilocks making some bacon.then goldilocks ran out the dore. and we fownd the cops.and then the cops cot her and took her to jail. and she stade there for 20 years.

Writing from an Idea Bank

In January in Surrey, B.C., it had still not snowed. The children were wishing for snow, and the teacher brainstormed for what they might do if it ever did snow. Their wishes were recorded on the chalkboard. The children grouped all the rhyming words together, and the teacher modeled internal rhyme. This was a combination grade one and two.

Jeremy in grade one wrote:

> I wish it would snow
> I would play in the snow
> I would sleigh in the snow
> I would lay in the snow
> I would stay in the snow
> I would hop in the snow
> I would stop in the snow
> I would flop in the snow
> I would plop in the snow
> I wish it would snow.

Elaine in grade two wrote:

> I wish it would snow.
> I would play in the snow.
> I would sleigh in the snow.
> I would lay in the snow.
> I would stay in the snow.
> I would fall in the snow.
> I would call in the snow.
> I would haul in the snow.
> I would play ball in the snow.
> I would ride in the snow.
> I would glide in the snow.
> I would hide in the snow.
> I would roll in the snow.
> I would pull in the snow.
> I would bowl in the snow.
> I would dig a hole in the snow.
> I would sleep in the snow.
> I would creep in the snow.
> I wish it would snow.

All of the children created similar lists.

From grade one at the end of January after studying and making an idea bank about whales, the following writings were typical. One of the least skilled papers read:

> Big slow whales eat at Seaworld
> Gray slow whales sound in the blue water

(The spelling was all correct; the child had copied from the idea bank. The handwriting was shaky and there were no periods.) Two average papers were:

> I like big killer whales under the water.
> Little white whales sing in the ocean.

Black nar whales do tricks in the sea.
Big pilot whales dive under the water.
Fast killer whales sing in warm water.
Are whales warm?

One of the most skilled papers was:

Pilot slow whales dive in salt water
Look at the pilot whales swiming in the salt
water
I see the pilot whales swiming in the water
do you see them
yes I do see the pilot whales swiming in the water
I do to. I like the pilot whales. pilot whales
haf bluber and sum whales go fast and sum are nice
I like the nice whales
I like it wen whales dive in the water. I like
wacen the whales dive be cuse it's fun wacen.

(The spelling was not always correct because this child was writing without reference to the chalkboard, or the idea bank, although it was available. With so much to say, there is less attention for a while to the mechanics. This writing wasn't nagged by the teacher. Periods and capital letters will be nagged and corrected.)

7

Poetry and Song

Poetry is meant to be heard. Its rhythm and cadences and its rhyme, if any, make it a natural vehicle for introducing children to print. The oral comes first, the reciting by the teacher and children. The text of poems may be held in place by a single picture representing a line or phrase or by the actual words.

Robert chose to solve the mystery of print from "Disobedience" rather than *Winnie-the-Pooh*. He knew *Winnie* well, but he did not have the exact memorization for any chapter of *Winnie*. The length of any one chapter makes memorization more difficult, but Robert knew all of Milne's poetry, two full books, so it was not length that made him choose. It is the poet's careful choice of words demanded by the cadence and form that makes a poem so exactly predictable that it is memorized perfectly much more easily than prose. Many of the prose selections that we recommend for introducing children to print in picture books are poetic in all respects except that the print is not set in stanza form.

Nursery Rhymes

Nursery rhymes are a natural vehicle for bringing children to language. They contain all the cadences of spoken English in short stanzas, enticing children to chant them over and over. The rhythm and the fun of the rhymes make them easy for all children to learn. We teach all the children the rhymes in kindergarten, chanting them many times and working with the ideas through art and drama. In this we provide the opportunity for all children to understand the rhymes and to memorize them.

We can now use the familiar rhymes at the beginning of grade one to teach children concepts about print. We teach from many rhymes but will only detail a few here, using each rhyme to develop a particular concept. We develop concepts about both print and meanings.

Developing the Concept of a Printed Word and Sequencing Speech

We say the rhyme "One, Two, Buckle My Shoe" to make sure that all the children know the words. After four or five chantings, we place the numerals in the pocket chart as we say the complete rhyme. We place two numerals in each line:

1	2
3	4
5	6
7	8
9	10

We then ask the children to listen and watch as we repeat the first line of the rhyme, indicating the numerals and then three spaces in the pocket chart as we say, "1, 2, Buckle my shoe." The children are asked if anything is missing. If the children respond, "No," we repeat the chanting and tracking, telling the children to watch and listen, until some child realizes that some words are missing.

We then need to ascertain how many words are missing. Many beginning grade-one children do not understand what a *word* is. First-grade children have told us that *buckle my shoe* was one, two, three, four, and eight words. We have the children tell what the first word is, the second, and the third, helping all children to begin to understand.

We have the words *Buckle* and *my*, and a picture of a shoe on cards:

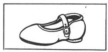

We show the children the cards, help them to discern which card says what, and have them place the cards in the pocket chart, helping if needed. We begin with the picture of the shoe. We ask a child to select the card that says *shoe* from the three cards and to place it in the pocket chart where it should go. If the card is placed at the end of the line, we ask, "Why did you put it there?" to develop the idea that it should go at the end of the first line leaving room for *Buckle* and *my*.

Usually the shoe picture is placed beside the 2 card with no space for *Buckle* and *my*. We point and chant, "1, 2, shoe," although most children say, "1, 2, Buckle my shoe." We repeat, pointing to emphasize the **one word–one card** relationship. We have frequently had to do this several times before some child suggests that *shoe* goes at the end of the line. Confusion about what a printed word is is normal, and most children need lots of help and lots of repetition of activities to sort out this basic notion.

Now we have the children apply simple phonics to figure out which card says *Buckle* and which says *my* and then place them in the right place in the pocket chart. We wait if there is difficulty, "forcing" the children to discover the proper placement. Sometimes the teacher has to point to the blank spaces as everyone chants the line several times. We finish the first line. We read the first line together while pointing to each word and go on to the second line, discovering that three words are missing in that line. We redo the exercise of getting the words placed. We build the entire rhyme in the pocket chart, reading each new line as we add it and predicting the words that should be next. We may teach this same lesson two or three times on subsequent days. We will teach similar lessons with other rhymes to redevelop the same concepts of word and sequence.

Small groups of children can now practice with the word cards, mixing them, then placing them in correct order, either on the floor or in the pocket chart.

Using the Structure of a Rhyme to Write a New Poem
We chant or sing the rhyme "Polly Put the Kettle On."

> Polly put the kettle on,
> Polly put the kettle on,
> Polly put the kettle on,
> We'll all have tea.

We build the first line in the pocket chart using one card for each word. We point to each word and chant. We give the children the words for the second and third lines and have them build the second and third lines in the pocket chart. They are required to match underneath to do this step. We build the fourth line as we did *Buckle my shoe* and *Shut the door*, having the children apply phonics to figure out the placement of the word cards.

After several practices in "reading" the rhyme as the teacher tracks the words, we replace the *Polly* with the children's names, one name on each card. This provides lots of chanting and tracking practice because the teacher must change the name cards until every child's name has been used.

The next step is to brainstorm for things that can be put on:

on the table	on yourself in summer
on the stove	on yourself for baseball
on yourself to play	on yourself for hockey
on yourself in winter	

We use one for a heading to list the responses on the chalkboard. For *on the table* we might get:

forks	bread
knives	cookies
salt	glasses
pepper	milk
spoons	

We use these to build such parodies as:

Harry put the forks on,
Sally put the knives on,
Kerry put the spoons on,
And wash your hands for dinner.

We build several parodies, and we use other rhymes to build parodies.

Developing Sequence

We make a series of pictures to represent the lines of rhymes such as "Little Miss Muffet," one picture for each line:

Little Miss Muffet
Sat on a tuffet
Eating her curds and whey.
Along came a spider
That sat down beside her,
And frightened Miss Muffet away.

We have the children arrange the pictures in sequence in the pocket chart, one picture per line. We have a set of numeral cards, 1 through 6. We tell the children we are making a puzzle as we rearrange the cards in the pocket chart in some random order. We pass out the numeral cards and have the children place the numeral one by the picture of *Little Miss Muffet*, the numeral two by the picture of *a tuffet*, etc. (see fig. 15).

We can do the same sort of sequencing with any nursery rhyme for which we have pictures.

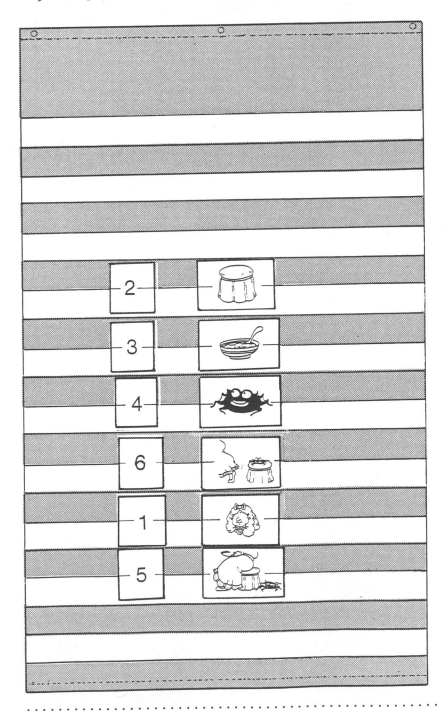

FIGURE 15. Numbering the pictures for "Little Miss Muffet"

Developing Rhyme

We build "A Hunting We Will Go" in the pocket chart as we did "Polly Put the Kettle On," using pictures for *fox* and *box:*

> A-hunting we will go,
> A-hunting we will go,
> We'll catch a [fox]
> And put him in a [box],
> A-hunting we will go.

After the rhyme has been learned, we turn the pictures around so that *fox* and *box* are blank spaces. We choose animal names that have many rhymes, and we place them on the chalkboard as headings for columns as we brainstorm for rhyming words:

cat	dog	whale	goat	bear	deer	snake
mat	frog	sale	boat	stair	ear	lake
hat	log	pail	coat	fair	spear	cake
rat	fog	jail	float	pear	gear	bake
fat	bog	hail	moat	hair	steer	steak
brat	smog	fail	throat	chair	fear	rake

Orally we now use these words to create forty or more verses so that children understand how to use this rhyme bank:

> We'll catch a whale
> And put it in jail
>
> We'll catch a whale
> And feed him from a pail
>
> We'll catch a whale
> And put him up for sale

> We'll catch a bear
> And brush and comb his hair
>
> We'll catch a bear
> And take him to the fair
>
> We'll catch a bear
> And put him in a chair

If we cannot make a sensible rhyme with a word we skip it. Each child can create a verse and illustrate it. The pages can be made into a "big book" for all to sing and enjoy all year.

We can use the same rhyming list with "Baa, Baa, Black Sheep," substituting for the last two lines.

> Baa, baa, black sheep,
> Have you any wool?
> Yes sir, yes sir,
> Three bags full.
> One for my master,
> One for my dame,

But none for the little boy
Who cries in the lane.

But none for the cat that sits on the mat.
But none for the dog that is lost in the fog.
But none for the whale that is sitting in jail.

Developing the Understanding of Prepositions

We build "Little Bo Peep" as we did "1, 2, Buckle My Shoe" in the pocket chart:

Little Bo Peep
Has lost her sheep
And doesn't know where
To find them.
Leave them alone
And they will come home
Bringing their tails behind them.

We ask the children where the sheep might be and list all the suggestions on the chalkboard. We put the phrase *Are the sheep* on the chalkboard and have the children read their phrases as complete questions as we record them. We chant two or three questions each time we record a new one, drilling the print form of the ideas that are accumulating on the chalkboard.

Are the sheep
   in the meadow?
   over the mountains?
   under the bridge?
   behind the barn?
   near the freeway?

We list many responses and then put the children into pairs to illustrate the suggestions. The pairing causes discussion of the preposition and generally results in a much better quality illustration. We put all the illustrations into a "big book," labeling each picture with a full question (Are the sheep in the school house?) and the answer, "No, no, no," until the last page, where we say, "Yes, yes, yes." Similarly we can use "Mary Had a Little Lamb" to brainstorm places where Mary went and the lamb followed and "Little Boy Blue" to brainstorm where else the cows and sheep might roam.

Song Lyrics as Writing Structures

Practicing with Words, Letters, and Syllables

As a beginning activity we can use the song "Here We Are Together" in classification activities that give the children practice in working with words, syllables, letters, and letter sounds.

We make name cards for each child and place the words to the song "Here We Are Together" in the pocket chart as follows:

Oh, here we are together, together, together.
Oh, here we are together, together we'll stay.
There's _____ and _____
and _____ and _____.
Oh, here we are together, together we'll stay.

We put the song in the pocket chart and add four names as we sing the song. We sing it again and add four other names. After several days of practice so that every child's name has been used many times, we give the name cards to the children. In kindergarten we give each child his or her own name, but in first grade we hand out the cards randomly. The entire class now sings the song and individual children take the solo parts by singing the name of the card that they have been given.

Children can practice further by sorting the name cards. They may sort the cards many ways. For example:

Names that they know, and those they do not know
Names that are long, and those that are short
Names that begin with the same letter
Names that have an *e,* an *m,* etc., in them
Names that have one, two, three, or more beats in them
Names of boys and names of girls

Sorting cards is a valuable activity at beginning reading levels. It leads the children to look closely at the printed word, and it shows the teacher what the children know or do not yet know about words and letters.

We use lots of songs as structures upon which to put our ideas. We use songs the children have sung over and over again to the point that the melody and rhythm are within them. They then do not have to think much about the structure but can put their full effort into what they are saying. For example, "The Farmer in the Dell" is marvelous for beginning writing because it has such delightful repetition, giving children the needed practice in writing. "Farmer in the Dell" has resulted in the following writing:

The wolf ate grandmama.
The wolf ate grandmama.
Oh my, she's going to die.
The wolf ate grandmama.

The wolf ate Red Riding Hood.
The wolf ate Red Riding Hood.
Oh my, she's going to die.
The wolf ate Red Riding Hood.

Charlotte spun a web.
Charlotte spun a web.
Wilbur was a terrific pig
When Charlotte spun a web.

We have used "Sing a Song of Sixpence" as a structure. This is a more sophisticated structure than it may seem at first so that we tend to use it from grade two on. We have used it to restate such content as the Big Mac commercial:

Sing a song of Big Mac
Sesame bun,
Two all beef patties,
Very well done.
Onions, pickles, lettuce,
Cheese and special sauce.
Please don't burp and please don't slurp,
Or mother will be cross!

For pizza lovers we have composed:

Sing a song of pizza,
Mozzarella cheese.
Put on lots of bacon,
Some anchovies, please.
When the pizza's baked,
We all begin to eat.
Isn't that a gooey dish
To carry down the street?

The song examples do not just take place by telling the children to write a song. The song has to be one that they know well. The content they are to render into song has to be well known. (We are merely repeating the requisites of writing.) The teacher has to model the responses with the children. She might begin by asking, "What foods could we sing a song of?" One child responds, "Ice cream." Another responds, "Vegetables." A third says, "Ketchup." The teacher sings several with the children:

Sing a song of ice cream . . .
Sing a song of vegetables . . .
Sing a song of ketchup . . .
Sing a song of beans . . .

With the singing of beans she draws the children's attention to the distortion of be-eens as demanded by the two syllables of "Sixpence." The teacher then writes on the chalkboard:

Sing a song of _____ beans . . .

She elicits *string, green, yellow, lima, pinto, refried,* etc. She leads the class in singing each version and the class decides which sounds best.

> Sing a song of string beans
> Growing on the vine
> Some are green and some are yellow
> They all taste very fine.
> Snap them, cut them, shred them
> Put them on a plate
> You better come to dinner on time
> They'll be eaten if you're late.

The teacher will need to lead and model the process of writing several times. She follows the children's ideas, encourages them to lead and create, and provides the leadership if the children falter. After the modeling, the pupils work in groups of four to six to create their versions, and, as they gain facility, they create songs individually.

"I've Been Working on the Railroad" is another song that is fairly easy to work with. We suggest to children that they become someone, a witch at Halloween, Santa Claus, Charlotte in *Charlotte's Web,* etc., and help the class create several first lines:

> I've been working at the cauldron
> I've been working at the North Pole
> I've been working by the barn door

The teacher questions to help children follow the song pattern, asking, "When have you been working?" This elicits the second line, and of course the third line is a repeat of the first. The development usually is one version at a time, but occasionally two or three might be developed simultaneously. All of the lyrics are recorded by the teacher on the chalkboard and revised and revised so that children can see print functioning. The teacher pushes children for veracity when they are Charlotte so that the song becomes a book review of sorts:

> I've been working at the barn door
> From dusk to early dawn
> I've been working at the barn door

The teacher asks, "Why have you been working?" if necessary, and elicits several responses, trying each response within the song as everyone sings, repeating the first three lines each time. This rehearsal is a necessary part of language play in creating song parodies for most children. They have learned a total structure and rarely can begin in the middle even when singing the original. The teacher elicits:

> To spell "some pig" just right
> To save young Wilbur's life

> To help keep Wilbur alive
> To deceive Mr. Zuckerman

The teacher asks, "What happens in the morning when they see *some pig?*" and elicits endings such as:

> Can't you hear the people gasping
> When they read SOME PIG
> Can't you hear Zuckerman a-boasting,
> "Wilbur is some pig!"

> Once the people have read "some pig"
> I'll need another word
> I'll need Templeton to fetch it
> Because I don't spell well.

Sometimes we put the full lyric of the original song in the pocket chart, one word per card, and sing it and clap the rhythm to focus upon the syllabic needs. We tend not to press for rhyme because, when we do, sense tends to disappear, and we get trite, forced rhyme. We work with sense and rhythm first and then sometimes modify our word choice or word order to achieve rhyme. With the song in the pocket chart, we create the parody by turning over words, usually one at a time, although sometimes a phrase, and then create a version that goes on top by printing words on additional word cards. This writing-on-top sometimes enables children to work with less teacher questioning because the lines being worked on are intuitively responded to as if they were teacher's question. For example, in "I've Been Working on the Railroad" the second line, "all the live-long day," tells when, and the children tend to create answers which tell "when" without being asked or directed.

We use song parodies using children's ideas, using the content of literature, and to work in areas of social studies and science. For example, we use "She'll Be Coming round the Mountain" in social studies focusing upon one particular locality, state, or country. For New Mexico we have had such verses as:

> She'll be coming to New Mexico today
> [etc., as the first verse, followed by:]
> She'll see pueblos and clay ovens when she comes.
> She'll hear Spanish being spoken when she comes.
> She'll see mesas, buttes, and deserts when she comes.

Children have also used "This Land Is Your Land" to create such verses as:

> This land is my land, this land is your land
> From the Arizona border to the Texas badlands
> From the Rio Grande waters to the Colorado mountains
> This land was made for you and me.

As I was walking through the Santa Fe plaza
I saw the Indians selling their jewelry
I saw the red chilies hanging in bunches
I knew that I was in New Mexico

After studying North America, children began to study other countries, creating parodies such as:

This land is my land
This land is your land
From the English Channel
To the Riviera
From the Bay of Biscay
To the Swiss border
This land was made for you and me.

As I was walking through the streets of Paris
I saw before me the Eiffel Tower,
The Arc of Triumph
The Bourbon Palace,
Landmarks of fame in my country.
[Tom McKenna and John Muhlberger, Grade 6 social studies report]

Poetry as Writing Patterns

Poetry is parodied in a similar fashion. First it must be memorized. Until the cadence is in the children, the writing of parodies is difficult. Usually we have the original poem in the pocket chart on word or phrase cards, depending upon the length and complexity of the poem and the grade level of the children we are teaching. For beginning grades we tend to have each word on a separate card, and for older children we tend to work in phrases.

We use very simple poetry such as David McCord's "Notice"[1] and have children write in a slightly adapted version. This exercise is just like frame sentences. We have the children substitute other animals and tell where the animal is in the last line, creating such poems as:

I have a tarantula
I have an asp
I have a boa constrictor
Wrapped around my leg.

I have a duck
I have some geese
I have some sheep
Under my seat.

1. David McCord, "Notice," in *One at a Time* (Boston: Little, Brown, 1974).

I have a bat.
I have a cat.
I have a spider.
Ready for Halloween.

We have used a pattern from Margaret Wise Brown:

Little Old Toad
Little Old Toad
Where have you been?
I've been way up the road
Said Little Old Toad
That's where I've been.[2]

We read several of her poems orally and provide one in the pocket chart as a model, and in a second pocket chart or on the chalkboard, we provide the writing model:

Little Old _____
Little Old _____
Where have you been?
I've been _____
Said Little Old _____
That's where I've been.

This poem has a rhyme scheme, and we help children with rhyme by creating a "rhyming chart." The teacher begins by suggesting to children the names of animals for which there are many rhymes. We brainstorm for words that rhyme with the animals, creating a "rhyming word bank" such as the one that follows:

goat	whale	ox	goose	raccoon	cat
boat	jail	box	moose	spoon	mat
moat	pail	flocks	spruce	June	bat
note	mail	clocks	juice	moon	flat
float	sale	fox	papoose	soon	slat
coat	stale	rocks	noose	baboon	hat
vote	quail	locks	reduce	croon	rat
wrote	hail	stocks	loose	loon	vat
quote	rail	knocks	Bruce	tune	gnat

With rhyme taken care of, children can now concentrate on making sense. The teacher models with the class, and orally they create a dozen

---

2. Margaret Wise Brown, *Where Have You Been?* (New York: Hastings House, 1952).

or more verses. We practice many possibilities for one animal. For
example, using *goat,* we have the following possibilities:

> I've been riding in a boat
>> swimming across the moat
>> writing myself a note
>> sitting on the float
>> trying on a coat
>> registering to vote

We have used Karla Kuskin's "If I Were a...." It contains four
stanzas, each following the same pattern.

> If I were a bird
> I would chirp like a bird
> With a high little cry.
> I would not say a word.
> I would sit on my nest
> With my head on my chest,
> Being a bird.[3]

From this, children have written such other versions as:

> If a were a coyote,
> I would sit on the rock
> In the high hills of Texas
> And howl at the night
> At the big yellow moon.
> I would run slyly
> To catch my prey,
> Being a coyote.
>
> [Randy Dalaba, Grade 3]

> If I were a stream,
> I would noisily run into a roaring river.
> I would have fish swim quickly in me.
> I would have little kids wade all day long,
> Being in a stream.
>
> [Butch Cleve, Grade 3]

> If I were a zebra,
> I'd run through the woods.
> I'd eat juicy green grass.
> I'd hide from wild lions.
> I'd sleep on a grassy hill.
> I'd jump and run
> Being a zebra.
>
> [Jorge Peres, Grade 3]

3. Karla Kuskin, "If I Were a...," in *Dogs and Dragons, Trees and Dreams* (New York:
Harper, 1980).

If I were a square dance,
I would keep the beat
While the people clapped
And stomped their feet,
While the caller called
And the musicians played,
Being a square dance.

[J. J. Day, Grade 3]

Memorizing Poetry

We may begin with children just coming to reading with very short rhymes such as "I Like Bugs" by Karla Kuskin.

I am very fond of bugs.
I kiss them
And I give them hugs.[4]

We print each word on a word card and put the cards in the pocket chart as we recite the poem. Then we tell the children to close their eyes; we turn over one card and ask them to tell us the word that we turned over. They close their eyes; we turn over another word; they figure out what the word is; we continue until the whole poem is turned over. The children recite the poem from memory as the teacher points to each blank card. Sometimes after identifying the blank, for example *kiss*, we ask the children how they will know if they are right. "What letter should *kiss* begin with? end with?" We turn over the card to see if the word begins with *k* and ends with *s*. This is an application of phonics in word recognition. Words should be spelled with the letters we expect, even if there are some extra letters or unexpected spellings.

Older children enjoy this turning-over technique. A poem is presented totally on the chalkboard or overhead. The teacher has the poem on individual word cards; he or she erases the chalkboard and passes out the word cards randomly, giving each child an equal number of words insofar as possible. The class is challenged to recreate the poem in the pocket chart. Usually a class is able to do this for an eight- to ten-line stanza. If the class needs help, the teacher rereads the whole poem orally with the class reading together those parts that are already in the pocket chart.

The poem is read together several times to work on choral expression and to practice differing intonations as suggested by the students or teacher. Now the teacher says, "Close your eyes," and turns over one or two words. The class recites the whole line while the teacher points. Eventually all the words are turned over, and the teacher points as the

---

4. Karla Kuskin, "I Like Bugs," in *Dogs and Dragons, Trees and Dreams* (New York: Harper, 1980).

class recites. In a matter of one lesson, thirty to fifty minutes, ten lines are learned. We begin the next day with the word cards distributed randomly, and we review the poem. Thereafter, the cards become a challenge for an individual or small group to sequence.

We use a similar technique with older children. We put each word of a poem on a separate card. We include capital letters and punctuation next to the words on the word cards. We give a stanza to four to six children and ask them to see if they can figure out what the poem says. (We may demonstrate this in the pocket chart by putting all the words in the chart randomly and working with the whole class to recreate the original text.) For longer poems we sometimes put phrases instead of individual words on sentence strips. In the process of recreating a poem, the poem is partially or totally memorized. A second or third recreating may be necessary to fix perfect memory. Sometimes we put a four- to six-stanza poem on cards and distribute the whole poem, one stanza to each of six groups within a class, and set them to solving the individual stanzas. When the stanzas are sorted, the job becomes one of deciding the sequence of the stanzas. Again, this focus on meaning, on syntax and cadence causes children to attend so intently that most of the poem is memorized. The solved poem cards go into envelopes for children to take later for another recreation.

Poetry for Reading Prediction

We use poetry for total class reading and prediction. We make a transparency to project each stanza. First we present the title alone and talk about it, speculating about the content of the poem. The poem is covered with two sheets of paper which are manipulated so that the words of the poem can be exposed as if we were writing, one letter at a time. The pupils predict what the word being exposed is and the next word or phrase. As fast as the words are predicted, they are exposed. We reread orally that part of the poem that has been exposed over and over, forcing the natural flow of language to aid prediction. The teacher helps the pupils by asking questions to guide their predictions, since she knows what is coming next. For example we have used "Think of It" by Bette Killion:

> "Go quickly," says my mother
> or some other hurry person.
>   Then I think of fast things—
>   hummingbird wings
>   lizards darting
>   racers starting
>   bicycle wheels

automobiles
wind through the trees
some angry bees—
and I'm quick!

"Sh-h-h," says my mother
or some other tiptoe person.
    Then I think of still things—
        empty swings
        dark nights
        soaring kites
        thick, soft mittens
        newborn kittens
        whispered prayers
        sleeping bears—
    and I'm quiet!

"Slow down," says mother
or some other
getting tired person.
    Then I think of lazy things—
        yawning kings
        elephants strolling
        plump pigs rolling
        a cow chewing cud
        some oozing mud
        inchworm on my hand
        sifting sand—
    and I go slow![5]

We expose the title and author and read them aloud. Next we expose merely the first quotation mark and ask, "What is happening?" eliciting the response that someone is talking. Now we expose only the *G*, asking, "What do you think someone is saying?" We take a few responses, and if we get *go* we expose the word immediately; if not we slowly expose the *o*. Now we ask, "How are you to go?" The questioning is crucial to the predicting. The questioning is done to reduce the possible answers. *How are you to go* creates the possibility of *quickly; when* or *where are you to go* eliminates *quickly* as a response. The questioning does not guarantee the author's exact word, but it increases its likelihood. However, the efficacy of this technique is not dependent upon correct answers. The technique uses the intuitive responses of children to the sound of language plus attention to meaning. This anticipatory

---

5. Bette Killion, "Think of It," in *Poetry Place Anthology* (New York: Instructor Publications, 1983).

set, this apprehension, is what is basic to language acquisition and comprehension.

After five or six responses we expose *quickly* letter by letter if we have not had *quickly* as a response. Usually the exposing of the letter *q* results in *quickly* if it has not already been given. We expose the comma and the end of the quotation mark, asking, "What has happened?" establishing that the person has stopped talking. We read orally the part already exposed, *Go quickly.* Almost always this results in several children saying, "Said," so we expose *sa* and say, "Not quite." If we do not get *says*, we expose the *y* and finally the whole word, *says.* We reread orally, "*Go quickly,*" *says* and ask, "Who might tell you to go quickly?" Almost always one of the responses will be correct, so we expose *mother* and reread orally asking, "Who else?" quickly establishing the phrase *or some other hurry person* by letter-by-letter exposure. We read the first sentence orally once or twice chorally.

We reread the title and the first sentence and we ask, "What do you do?" pushing to get someone to use the title as we expose *Then.* We continue, establishing the line *Then I think of fast things.* We interrupt the poem to predict the fast things that we might think of. Sometimes we list these on the chalkboard. Sometimes we merely list them in the air. We make sure that the fast thing is fast. For example children have frequently responded *airplanes.* Our response may be, "When? Airplanes sometimes sit on the runway." The child may respond, "Airplanes flying," and again we push by asking, "Is anything faster than flying?" eliciting, perhaps three or more responses such as *soaring, diving, roaring, or screeching.*

We have occasionally gotten the response *hummingbirds,* and push for *wings* by asking, "What part is the fastest?" Our goal is not to get the exact words, but whenever it is fairly simple to get the exact words we do, treating them as we do all responses. After twenty or more responses, we begin exposing the words of the poem.

We do the same sort of thing with stanza two. Children sense the repeated pattern, and their predictions are quicker and more accurate. We complete the third stanza. Now two activities are possible for practicing from the poem. We can pass out word and phrase cards for the poem, putting the *fast things,* the *still things,* the *lazy things* on phrase cards, and recreate each stanza in the pocket chart, using the "close your eyes" technique as we turn over the cards. We can have more than one set of cards for use, so that groups of four can be given a card set and asked to solve which stanza they have and to see if they can sequence it.

Writing follows naturally using the poem as a structure. We can recreate the poem, substituting for the author's *fast things* from our brainstormed predictions, and from our *still* and *lazy* brainstorming. We can change the beginning of the poem to *Come quickly,* and recreate the poem using ideas demanded by *come.* We can change the person to brother, sister, or father, or policeman, teacher, or scientist.

We recommend teaching and memorizing a poem a week, although not all may be retained for the year. We frequently place one of the memorized poems of last month in the pocket chart face down and challenge the children to figure out from the pattern which poem it is and to remember the exact words.

8

Paragraph Writing

$\mathbf{W}$e work with paragraph writing with children as soon as they have reasonable command of sentence writing and can spell with ease. This means the middle of grade one for a few children and the beginning of grade two for almost all. We tend to teach paragraph writing in groups of eight or ten, although it can be done with the whole class. Not all pupils may be able to do the final step of writing paragraphs independently, even though they are able to participate orally and in group writing.

We do not define what a paragraph is, except to teach the mechan ical parts of indentation and consecutive sentence writing. Essentially pupils come to understand that a paragraph is a list stated in sentence form with the first line indented.

Technique 1

We choose a topic that the children know something about. Commonly we choose an animal or a TV character. We brainstorm, asking the children, "Tell me what you know about bears." As the children respond, we record their responses in phrases on the chalkboard:

have four feet	some are white
stand on hind feet	eat fish
can run fast	babies called cubs
brown and black	big bears don't climb trees
eat berries	cubs climb
like salmon	have short tails
eat garbage in dumps	hibernate
are very big	can learn tricks

```
eat honey                    like to eat bugs and grubs
have fur
```

We help in getting the ideas organized by asking the pupils if they see any two ideas that go together. Sometimes we put the information on sentence strips so that we can physically put the strips together in the pocket chart. Sometimes we ask a question to help organize the ideas. For example, "What do bears eat?" yields the following phrases:

```
eat berries
 eat fish
like salmon
eat garbage in dumps
eat honey
like to eat bugs and grubs
```

We work with the children orally to develop sentences which join the ideas. The most common conjunction is the overworked *and*. We use it, but we provoke other conjunctions whenever we can. We teach the use of commas in a series if the children do not know it, so that we get the following sentences as a minimum:

Bears eat berries, bugs, and grubs.

Bears eat almost everything. They eat berries, bugs, grubs, salmon, other fish, honey, and even eat garbage from garbage dumps.

We strive to join ideas more maturely in our instructional sessions, hoping that the children will learn from the modeling and reflect it in their writing. Together we write:

Bears eat almost anything. They eat bugs, grubs, honey, fish, especially salmon, and berries, even raiding garbage dumps at campgrounds for all sorts of bread, vegetables, and junk food.

This last example is unlikely without lots of teacher prodding and questioning, but it is possible. It is only after lots of oral work with the teacher helping that the written work will take on the same maturity.

We continue questioning, "What other items might go together?" Pupils suggest:

```
cubs climb
big bears don't climb trees
```

We might suggest adding *baby bears called cubs* to help the pupils create:

The baby bears, called cubs, climb trees, but the big bears don't.

We may ask what word could be substituted for *big* and get *grown up, mature, and adult;* we use all three in different sentence models:

Adult bears don't climb trees, but cubs do.
Bear cubs climb trees but when they mature they no longer climb trees.
Baby bears climb trees, but grown up bears do not.

Children will give many suggestions that are similar. The teacher accepts all oral sentences and records those that have some phrase or quality to highlight. Frequently the way to get mature sentences is to get the children to combine the best of two or three oral sentences. This pushing for quality in sentence structure is particularly important with older children.

We make additional combinations of ideas to create more oral sentences, and we record the one we like best on the chalkboard. We discuss what we shall say first about bears, and with the teacher pointing, the class chorally reads several sentences. We try varying sentence orders, and we build the sequence in the pocket chart using the phrase strips to help us remember the sequences.

The teacher finally writes one or more versions of the paragraph on the chalkboard as the children dictate by reading chorally. Some children need to see the full, finished paragraph before they sense what they need to do in writing. For some the oral work is sufficient.

One example is not sufficient to teach paragraph writing, so we repeat the procedures with a different content on another day, teaching paragraph writing several times before we expect children to work independently or in independent groups.

Technique 2

We read a short story, or we use a short story that we have read to the pupils several times. We say, "Tell me about Red Riding Hood." We record twenty or more phrases, as many as the children give, and then we say, "Which five are the most important?" We discuss and select five to eight phrases, since the children cannot always agree on exactly five. We put those selected onto sentence strips and ask if any go together, and why. We arrange them into some sequence and ask, "What do these tell you?" From the answers we create a topic sentence and then say the phrases in sentence form to build a paragraph.

If we like our paragraph we may write it on the chalkboard or on a chart; if not we will work some more orally with different sequences or elaborations until we have a good paragraph. Then we will write it for all to see. Most children need to see the paragraph created next to the phrase cards even though they have said the paragraph orally. This seeing of notes growing into paragraphs is necessary for children to get them to realize what an author does.

Technique 3

We write in imitation of an author. We present children with a full paragraph on the overhead, on chart paper, or in the pocket chart. Usually the paragraph will be one that we have read to them orally. For example, in a grade-two class the teacher had read Ezra Jack Keats's *John Henry, an American Legend*. She chose the following excerpt to imitate:

> The sky swirled soundlessly round the moon.
> The river stopped murmuring.
> The wind stopped whispering
> and the frogs and the owls
> and the crickets fell silent—
> all watching and waiting and listening.[1]

The class discussed the meaning, the feelings, the mood, and the teacher suggested they change the paragraph to a noisy one. Together they created:

> The sky whirled around the moon.
> The wind whispered, then howled then growled.
> The frogs and owls and crickets all chirped
>   and talked loudly.
> The river began to overflow with a roar.

In grade three we have used a shortened paragraph from Felix Salten's *Bambi* where Bambi senses spring:

> The trees stood still under the blue sky. On the shrubs and bushes in the undergrowth the flowers unfolded their red, white, and yellow stars. Out of the earth came whole troops of flowers like motley stars, so that the soil of the twilit forest shone with silent, colorful gladness. Everything smelled of fresh leaves, and blossoms, and green wood. When the morning broke, the whole woods resounded with a thousand voices, and from morning till night, the bees hummed, the wasps droned, and filled the fragrant stillness with their murmur.[2]

We ask the children to read the paragraph silently to discover what time of year it is. Regardless of their answers we ask them to prove them,

1. Ezra Jack Keats, *John Henry, an American Legend* (New York: Pantheon, 1965).
2. Felix Salten, *Bambi* (New York: Pocket Books, 1979), p. 13.

and establish that it is spring. We then read the whole paragraph orally together and refer to each sentence in sequence to check understanding. We note the sense to which each sentence appeals and note that the author has begun with the sense of sight, then used smell, and finally hearing. We identify which words are the key words denoting spring and suggest that we rewrite the paragraph by changing to another season. We do this orally together and then have the children write individual versions. Near Halloween, third-grade children wrote the following paragraphs:

> The trees sway and swerve under stormy black skies. The bare branches and shrubs bend, scratch, and grab you. Out of the earth comes frost, fog, and mist. Everything smells of death. Leaves, twigs, flowers, ants, spiders, and ladybugs die and rot. When night falls, trees whistle, the witches cackle, the ghosts groan, the mummies moan, the werewolfs howl. The wicked sounds of the forest terrify you! [*Werewolfs* was the only spelling error.]

> The bare trees swished and swayed under the black clouds. The shrubs and bushes curled up in the cold air under the fir trees, hiding the vampires and ghosts. Out of the earth rise whole troops of witches, goblins, and skeletons. Bats hang from trees. Werewolves hide in the shadows. When the night falls, the woods resound with the frightening sounds of cackling, howling, booing, moaning, and groaning. It's Halloween.

Lloyd Alexander begins his novel *Time Cat* with a marvelous description of a cat:

> Gareth was a black cat with orange eyes. Sometimes, when he hunched his shoulders and put down his ears, he looked like an owl. When he stretched, he looked like a trickle of oil or a pair of black silk pajamas. When he sat on a window ledge, his eyes half-shut and his tail curled around him, he looked like a secret.[3]

We have children read the paragraph silently, and we discuss each sentence. We note that the first announces the animal with a brief physical description, and the following sentences tell a physical movement characteristic of cats and a simile to explain the movement. Now we can write an imitation, changing the animal and using three or more typical movements of that animal.

Bill Brittain in *Devil's Donkey* has Dan'l transformed into a donkey, and toward the end of the story Dan'l, as a donkey, is in a pulling match for his soul:

---

3. Lloyd Alexander, *Time Cat* (New York: Holt, 1963).

Suddenly Dan'l understood what it would be like never to be human again. And hard as his donkey's body was striving, he found himself thinking on all the things he'd be forsaking. The simple pleasure of talking to Jenny and being able to touch her with his words. The warmth of rich earth trod by bare feet, and the sleepy comfort of dozing in front of a fire when the wind blew raw outside. The tang of cold cider on a hot day, and the fluffy softness of a kitten's fur, and the miracle of watching a tiny seed grow to fullness in the sun and rain. All the joys of being human, the joys no animal could know.[4]

In this paragraph we note the recounting of simple pleasures in compound-sentence form. We brainstorm for our favorite things and simple pleasures. We expand each into full phrases by eliciting adverbial and adjective modifiers. For example, if a child says, "Ice cream," we ask, "What kind? How does it taste?" expanding the response to *delicious chocolate ice cream*. We extend further, asking, "Where is the delicious chocolate ice cream?" until we get a fully usable phrase, *delicious chocolate ice cream stacked on a double-dip cone*. Or we ask when you enjoy it most, and get the answer, *delicious chocolate ice cream on a toe-burning-pavement day*. Children substitute their own names for *Dan'l* and recreate the middle of the paragraph.

Similarly we have used Uncle C. C.'s peroration from Betsy Byars's *Good-bye, Chicken Little.*

"She demanded **meaning** when life is a **miracle**! Air to breathe, hundreds of vegetables, thousands of fruits, trees that turn green in the spring and red in the fall." His voice, high with excitement, made miracles of the things he mentioned. "Alaska **and** Florida. A sun **and** a moon. Oceans **and** deserts. Summer **and** winter."

He paused. He drew in a deep breath to calm himself. "And giraffes," he said finally.

"Giraffes?"

Uncle C. C. nodded. He had always had a fondness for the giraffe. He considered the giraffe a special comic miracle. It was as if God had said, "Look what I can throw in for good measure."

"And bears as white as the snow," he went on, "and horses black as night, and then little tiny sea horses that swim in the sea." He considered the sea horse another comic miracle.[5]

If we have read this book orally, the children know that Uncle C. C. is very old and talking about one of the other people in the old-folks home where he stays. We have the pupils read the excerpt silently, and then we read the selection chorally. We read it again chorally, this time eliminating all but Uncle C. C.'s monolog. We brainstorm and substitute

4. Bill Brittain, *Devil's Donkey* (New York: Harper, 1981), pp. 111–12.
5. Betsy Byars, *Goodbye, Chicken Little* (New York: 1979), pp. 71–72.

our own miracles, creating paragraphs beginning with *Life is a miracle!* imitating the dialog only.

The second paragraph of Patrick Keene Catling's book *The Chocolate Touch* is a list. We need only change the first sentence and the last slightly to get children to create new middles.

> He had only one bad fault: he was a pig about candy. Boiled candy, cotton candy, licorice all-sorts, old-fashioned toffee, candied orange and lemon slices, Cracker Jack, jelly beans, fudge, black currant lozenges for ticklish throats, nougat, *marron glacés,* acid drops, peppermint sticks, lollipops, marshmallows, and above all, chocolates—he devoured them all.[6]

We can change *candy* to *ice cream* or *pizza* or *vegetables.* We can change *he was a pig about candy* to *he was a nut about box tops. He saved* _____. Or *he was a nut about free offers in magazines. He wrote for* _____. This last paragraph is akin to Margaret Wise Brown's poem "Bugs," except that the form is different. We frequently challenge pupils to use a different structure to write the same information.

Technique 4

This is an extension of technique 2. We teach a content from two or three sources—sources that potentially may contradict each other. We brainstorm from each source and list phrase notes on sentence strips. If possible we view a film as well as read to the pupils. In studying about whales, for example, we may collect 100 or more facts over a period of two weeks. We have the pupils sort and resort the information into piles that go together. We may ask a question and have them put all the possible answers with the question in one pile. We organize the phrase cards and orally say the paragraphs; then the pupils write paragraphs in notebooks, in a sense creating their own texts. The following paragraph was written in remedial reading class by a grade-four child who was supposed to be having difficulty in reading. He was, but when he was interested in the content his persistence overcame much of his difficulty.

> Scientists believe that the whales lived on land a million years ago. And that their hind legs disappeared and their tail grew. The whale is the largest mammal that ever lived. Some whales are even bigger than the brontosaurus. Some blue whales are nearly one hundred feet long and weigh as much as one hundred tons. The blue whale is the largest one of them all.

6. Patrick Keene Catling, *The Chocolate Touch* (New York: Morrow, 1979).

Technique 5

We choose a topic—pirates, dinosaurs, any animal, or occupational groups of special interest, such as rock-and-roll stars or football players. With younger children we use the same technique with the Easter bunny, leprechauns, or Santa Claus. We brainstorm for answers to five or six questions, recognizing that there may be some overlap among the answers. We teach about the topic as we go along, so that we have a fairly large number of responses in each category. Eight answers is a minimum list.

About pirates we ask:

What are their names?
What do they look like?
What do they do?
Where do they live?
What do they have?
What do they wear?

We list the responses in six columns. A typical set of responses in grade two or three would be as follows if the teacher has taught from three or more sources:

Names	Look Like	Wear
Blackbeard	mean	bandanas
One-Eyed Jake	dirty	pantaloons
Captain Hook	fierce	black boots
The Red Beard	hawk-nosed	eye patches
Brothers	strong	earrings
Jacques LaFitte	powerful	three-cornered hats
Long John Silver	colorful	feathered hats
Dirty Dan	dangerous	striped shirts
Bluto	handsome	buckles on shoes
	ugly	gold rings

Have	Live	Do
swords	on board ships	steal
pistols	at the Ben Bow Inn	plunder
parrots	on deserted islands	fill the hold
lanterns	in caves	with plunder
shovels	above taverns	swab the deck
cannons	in New Orleans	hoist the sails
peg legs	on island in the	climb the rigging
hooks	Caribbean	fight

(Have)
treasure maps
flags with the
  Jolly Roger

(Do)
bury treasure
make treasure maps
sail the seas
hunt for ships
  to rob
hide on deserted
  islands
make people walk
  the plank
sleep in hammocks

We challenge the pupils to make up a story about a pirate, using at least one item from each column. We help by modeling orally at least one paragraph. Children tend to sequence in the order listed on the chalkboard, so we challenge them to say each paragraph in at least one other sequence. Again we model. We get such paragraphs as:

There was a pirate named One-Eyed Jake. He was hawk-nosed and mean. He wore pantaloons, black boots, and a three-cornered feathered hat. He had a pistol and a sword. He lived on his pirate ship and spent most of his days sailing the seas looking for ships to plunder.

Captain Hook was a mean pirate. He had a hook instead of a hand because the crocodile bit it off. He lived on a faraway island and on his ship. He spent his days looking for Peter Pan and worrying about the crocodile.

For grade-one children and others who seem unable to create a paragraph orally, we provide the help of a frame if we want to get these children into writing.

There was once a pirate named _____. He was _____ and _____. He wore _____ and _____. Wherever he went he took his _____ and his _____. _____ lived _____ and spent his days _____ and _____.

We have the children fill in orally, and then we try to get them to rearrange some of the sequence in an effort to move away from frame writing to freer writing. We find that children tend to choose work that is as difficult as they can handle, so that we do not push when children finally choose to use the frame.

Grade-one children in February brainstormed about villains and created the following stories using a similar frame:

There was once a villain named Janet the witch. She was weird and skinny. She wore old fashioned clothes and red capes. She lived in a scary house. She spent her days hanging people and giving poisonous needles.

There was once a villain named Sullivan Grundy. He was mean and gross. He wore a white coat and black pants. He lived in slippy mud. He spent his days shooting missles at people and chopping off heads.

There was once a villain named Werewolf. He was hairy and had sharp teeth. He wore ripped clothing and fur. He lived in a haunted mansion. He spent his days eating people.

Technique 6

We read a short story orally to the class, or we view a short film. We ask the children to brainstorm for the plot, or what one character did. We list all the responses on the chalkboard. We reread or see the film a second time if significant bits are missing. We put all the responses on a large sheet of butcher paper and on sentence strips. We use the sentence strips for organizing and selecting items.

We now ask the children to select the most important item from the list and to justify their choices. This usually results in a list of two to four responses. We work toward the most important by pairing the responses and telling the pupils to justify one as the more important. What we are getting is the main idea for a topic sentence to write a summary of the plot or the character's behavior. Sometimes we cannot select just one phrase as the most important, so we combine the phrases; this happens frequently because two or three of the phrases will be stating essentially the same idea using different words. We select six to ten of the items as most important and use these as notes to create a paragraph in the pocket chart. We recite the paragraph orally and then have the children write their individual versions.

We have used Farley Mowat's short story about Nicholai many times.

When I was a boy of twelve I was hunting with my grandfather. It was winter, and we had walked a long way from the village when we came to a thicket where many trees had been uprooted by a great wind. My grandfather stopped and sniffed the air like a dog.

"Ah," he said, "there is a big fellow sleeping close to here."

We went into the tangle and found a big mound. A tunnel half-filled with snow led into it.

"Well, boy, here is the bear's home. He is sleeping deep inside his house. I suppose we must leave him to his sleep, for what can one old man and one small boy do against a bear?"

He was challenging me. I took my knife out of my sheath, tested it on my thumb and said:

"What we can do is kill that bear!"

He smiled and put his gun down—it was an old muzzle loader. He took his hatchet and cut a long pole and sharpened one end of it. Then he scrambled up on the mound and shoved the pole downward with all his strength.

"Now I've tickled his ribs! Hand me my gun!"

I gave him the gun and he cocked it and pushed the barrel down the hole. It went off with a rumble like an earthquake—then there was a roar that made my skin go tight all over my body. My grandfather scrambled off the mound and we ran back to the edge of the wood while he reloaded his gun.

We waited but there were no more sounds from the house of the bear. After a while my grandfather uncoiled the halter rope he carried around his shoulders and tied a noose in one end of it.

"Now," he said, "we have another choice. We can go back to the village and get the strong young men to come here tomorrow and pull out that bear, or you can crawl down the tunnel yourself and tie the rope around him so we can pull him out together."

It was hard to make up my mind. I was very much frightened. I asked him to make the decision.

"That I cannot do," he said. "I am an old man and my life means nothing. You are young and your life means much, but it will mean very little if in the long run you cannot decide when to take risks with it."

He was telling me I could become a man on this day if I chose. I put the knife between my teeth and took the rope and crawled down the tunnel, pushing the snow out of the way with my shoulders.

It was too dark to see anything. I moved as slowly as I dared, but I knew if I stopped I would not start again. It stank in that tunnel and I could hardly breathe. There was no sound except the drumming of blood in my ears.

My hand touched something warm and I died a little. It was the paw of the bear. I lay there in the darkness for a long time and when I came to my senses I was stroking the bear's paw as if it was the head of a good dog. The paw never moved so I tied the loop around it and crawled out into the daylight. We pulled and we dug and we pulled and we dug for an hour before we got him out. Then we cleaned him and skinned him, and hung the meat in a tree out of the way of foxes. Finally we put his skull on the end of a pole and set it up above his house to honor his spirit and to calm his anger.

Then we went home. I was no longer a boy. I had become a man of the taiga, like all of those who had gone before me.[7]

We read it orally to pupils and brainstorm, asking them to tell about Nicholai. We got the following responses on one occasion:

---

7. Farley Mowat, *Siber, My Discovery of Siberia* (Toronto: McClelland & Stewart, 1973), pp. 111–12.

12 years old
went hunting with grandfather
carried knife
bragged he would kill bear with knife
went into den
tied rope on bear
took a risk
made a choice—a decision
became a man
helped pull out bear
stroked paw
helped skin bear
ran after shooting
was afraid and excited at the same time
learning how to hunt
learning to make decisions
challenged by grandfather
blood drummed in his ear
fainted
put skull on pole
bragged
held gun
cleared snow

We then asked the children which line was the most important. We do not expect consensus, and the children chose four answers as being the most important: *took a risk, made a choice—a decision, learning to make decisions,* and *became a man.* All of these focus on the same issue and resulted in a consensus statement: "Nicholai had to make a decision. It involved risk taking, and it resulted in his becoming a man."

Together the teacher and pupils expanded this to create an oral paragraph:

> When Nicholai was twelve he went bear hunting with his Grandfather. They shot the bear in its den, and Nicholai had to decide whether to crawl into the hole to tie a rope on the bear or to go home. He decided to crawl into the hole, and in getting the bear out became a man.

A day or two later we read orally the first chapter of Robert Newton Peck's *A Day No Pigs Would Die.*[8] We brainstormed about Rob and got the following responses:

ran away from school
ran away from Edward Thatcher

8. Robert Newton Peck, *A Day No Pigs Would Die* (New York: Knopf, 1972).

going to beat up Edward Thatcher
found Apron
beat Apron with a blackberry cone
tugged on Apron's calf
decided to get the calf born
took off his pants
ran through brambles
used his pants as a rope
tied pants to calf and tree
Apron licked Rob and calf
dragged down the hill
Apron bit Rob
kicked and dragged
became unconscious
grabbed something in Apron's throat
wasn't going to run away again

We recorded these on butcher paper as we did with Nicholai. We may again ask for the most important item and follow the procedures used with Rob, or we may choose to skip that and move on to character comparison. We hang the Nicholai notes next to the Rob notes and ask, "How are Rob and Nicholai alike?" If we have the phrase cards available, we can match directly from the cards. Usually we make the pairings by writing on the chalkboard. From these two sheets of notes we get the following likenesses:

decisions:	decided to get the calf born
	made a choice—a decision
tied animal:	tied pants to calf to tree
	tied rope on bear
took a risk:	grabbed something in Apron's throat
	went into the den
bragged:	going to beat up Edward Thatcher
	would kill the bear with his knife
lost consciousness:	fainted
	became unconscious

Next we create the topic sentence by asking, "What do those five pairs of ideas tell?" The most common response is, "How Rob and Nicholai are alike." We turn this into a declarative statement, "Rob and Nicholai were alike in several ways." We finish this orally, stating the ways, having several children create versions for each likeness. Now the pupils write their own versions. This results in paragraphs that are similar but unique. Obviously we can write how the boys were different, but tracing likenesses is more productive and usually more interesting to the pupils.

We continue with a third story a day or so later. We have used the Ray Bradbury story "Drummer Boy of Shiloh."[9] We also have used the films *Big Henry and the Polka Dot Kid, The White Heron,* and *Storm Boy.*[10] Each has a teenaged central character about whom we brainstorm. We now put up the brainstorming charts for Nicholai, Rob, and our next character, perhaps Sylvia in *The White Heron,* and ask, "How were Rob, Nicholai, and Sylvia alike?" One obvious likeness is Sylvia's making a decision not to tell the stranger where the white heron nested—a decision which results in Sylvia's maturing.

From these selections we raise the issue of decision making as risk taking and part of the process of maturing and growing up. This theme can be found in many short stories and novels; we ask the pupils to be alert for this and challenge them to find a novel or short story in which this happens. The teacher also searches for this theme, which is not restricted to juvenile novels, and models from adult books the kind of reporting expected from the pupils. Very briefly the teacher orally summarizes the novel, reading a paragraph or two that highlight decision making as a part of maturing. The children read individually, and two types of activities evolve. (1) Pupils do book reviews by making character comparisons. This is done orally, in written form, or both. (2) Discussion times are set for a group of six to eight pupils who each have found a book in which decision making has led to the maturing of a character. They sit together and report about their books. The pupils come prepared with a marked paragraph or two that demonstrate the decision making. Finding an appropriate excerpt is a difficult process for most children, even though they can cite the decision making well from memory.

9. Ray Bradbury, "Drummer Boy of Shiloh" in *Machineries of Joy* (New York: Simon & Schuster, 1964).

10. *Big Henry and the Polka Dot Kid, The White Heron,* and *Storm Boy* (Learning Corp. of America Films; distr. by Coronet/M.T.I., Deerfield, Ill.).

9

Research

A goal in education is to develop an inquiring mind and the skills to focus one's inquiries. Most children are natural scientists, concerned with the mysteries that surround them, and attend to the business of solving the mysteries if they know how. Research should be a matter of inquiry rather than a matter of format. Many children produce term papers that are supposed to be the result of study and inquiry but are unable to read them orally. Sometimes they understand the content, sometimes they do not. They have, however, created the papers themselves by copying paragraphs from several sources. They see research as a matter of format, and they have produced the format. They have not done any research because they do not know how and they do not understand what research is. We need to teach them how to collect information and how to organize. When they know how, children write papers that are honest research efforts.

In one sense research is nothing more than a series of organized lists. We start with a topic that we want to teach, having made sure that we have four or more sources for input and that the sources are in two or more forms. For example, to investigate spiders with a grade-five class we gathered materials. We located several spiderwebs outside the classroom, checking to make sure that the spiders were still there. We located several informational paragraphs and pages in *Charlotte's Web* by E. B. White;[1] we secured copies of *The Starfish Trilogy* by George Mendoza, *The Spider* by Margaret Lane, and *The Spider's Dance* by Joanne Ryder.[2]

---

1. E. B. White, *Charlotte's Web* (New York: Harper, 1952).
2. George Mendoza, *The Starfish Trilogy* (New York: Funk & Wagnalls, 1969); Margaret Lane, *The Spider* (New York: Dial Pr., 1982); Joanne Ryder, *The Spider's Dance* (New York: Harper, 1981).

We began with brainstorming, asking, "What do you know about spiders?" The children responded, and their answers were recorded on the chalkboard:

lay eggs
spin webs
have eight legs
eat flies
jump on bugs
make traps with a trap door
can't see well
fish for insects
use webs as traps

We take as many answers as we get and generally do not discuss the answers unless the children insist. For example, there were four children who thought the notion of *fishing for insects* was not true. We merely said, "It may not be so; we'll check as we study." (It was with great interest that the class confirmed the statement by discovering the *fishing* behavior of the bolas spider, although the bolas does not literally fish in water.)

Next we read orally from several pages of *Charlotte's Web,* a book that all the children knew. Most had not thought of the book as a source of information. We want children to know that authors of fiction usually describe background information as accurately as possible, so we use lots of nontextlike materials in gathering information. From *Charlotte's Web* several bits of information were added such as:

legs have seven sections
trochanter
tibia
coxa
tarsus
metatarsus
patella
legs are hairy
have two spinnerets
eat bugs, grasshoppers, gnats, midges, daddy longlegs, centipedes,
    mosquitoes, crickets [this was added to *eat flies,* which was
    already on the chalkboard]
put hundreds of eggs in one sack
dies after laying her eggs
etc.

From *The Spider's Dance,* a poetic narrative, was added:

fly by letting out draglines
speckled spiders hide under stones
grey spiders leap
yellow spider camouflages itself to hunt
live in cellars
live in attics
fireflies [added to the eating list]
birds eat spiders
can regenerate legs
sheds skin like a lobster as it grows

From *The Spider,* the class added:

have eight eyes
have two body parts
web is the strongest silk in the world
100,000 different spiders in the world
only some spin wheellike webs
oily feet so they don't stick in webs
jumping spiders stalk and pounce
eyes are in all parts of head
can see in several directions
crab spiders walk sideways and backwards
trap-door spider builds a hole with a trap door
some swim under water with an air bubble

From "To Spin a Silken Line or Two," the opening story in *The Starfish Trilogy,* we learned that not all spiders spin webs. This had been implied in Margaret Lane's book, but the children had been unable to make the inference because they thought all spiders spun webs. Apprehension is part of reading, a readiness, and the children were just not ready to infer something they thought was not true.

As we read to the children, they were told to listen for new information, for additional information to add to what was already on the chalkboard, and for corrections. The chalkboards eventually were filled with more than 100 bits of information.

We left the classroom, then, armed with individual chalkboards and chalk, went outside to observe the webs and the spiders in them. The children found the webs and were somewhat shocked to find that they were not wheellike but masses of threads shaped a bit like a cornucopia with the spider hidden deep in the bush at the end of the tunnel. We touched a web gently, and one spider came out quickly to investigate the wiggle, moving back almost instantly. We could induce no more spiders to come out by web wiggling; apparently we did not wiggle like a fly. Waiting patiently, we saw several spiders and counted eight eyes on each of them, two large eyes and six smaller ones. The legs had sections, but we could not count the seven. The children each sketched a web, and some sketched the spider.

Returning to the classroom we added a few more items to the chalkboard. It was time to organize our data. We needed to record it in a permanent, usable form, so we passed out blank sentence strips, one to each child. We pointed to the first item and asked a child to read it orally. We wanted to be certain that the child knew what he was to write. The child wrote with a felt pen on the sentence strip, using large enough letters so that the words could be read from a distance. We pointed to a second phrase and repeated the process. When a child finished one sentence strip he or she got another blank strip and waited to be assigned a second phrase to copy. Each child copied three or more phrases.

The material was organized in more than one way. One interesting classification that grew out of the spider work was a dichotomy: things that are true about all spiders and things that are true about some.

Most children need help in organizing, particularly if there is a lot of information. The easiest way is to ask a question, and to have the answers to that question put into one pocket of the pocket chart. For example, we asked, "What do spiders eat?" We consulted the pupils and labeled this group of cards "Eating Habits." We asked, "How do spiders catch their food?" and labeled the cards "Catching Food." We asked, "What do spiders look like?" and labeled this group "Appearance." We asked several questions and created several piles of strips within the chart, labeling each, in getting all the cards sorted. By labeling we created an unorganized table of contents and the headings of an outline. We organized the labels by putting the word *Spiders* on a card and putting it in the top of the pocket chart, saying, "All of the labels tell about spiders. If we were going to write a book about spiders, which category should we start with? What would be best next?" Etc.

Each label is a key word or phrase in any paragraph we write. We now take one of the stacks of cards, and together we create sentences and full paragraphs as described in chapter 8. The teacher leads in the writing of the paragraphs until he or she feels that the children are ready to write their own paragraphs.

The basic process may be used in teaching about any content. Each child may be expected to create several paragraphs and record these in a theme notebook and to add illustrations. Once this has been demonstrated as a group activity and the children have shown that they understand, they may begin to work individually and in small groups to study areas that they wish to research.

We teach one more bit of note taking before the children are expected to work independently. We make note pads by cutting paper into strips approximately three inches wide. We show children how to take the notes on the strips instead of on the chalkboard. We model the taking of notes, demonstrating how key words and phrases usually do not need to exceed one line. We show them that we draw a line under each note so that when all the note taking has been completed they can cut the strips into notes and have a set to organize as we did with the spider cards.

The process of learning to do research is extended in other ways. We do lots of mini-lessons as we begin the process of teaching children to do research. For example, each child picks a leaf from the same tree, or gets the same kind of weed stalk or leaf. In the classroom each child sketches the leaf as carefully as possible. Drawing requires attention to detail, and the more closely children have observed, the more responses we will get as we brainstorm about the leaf and its characteristics. The teacher circulates and comments as the children draw, using these comments to get the children to focus more fully upon the leaf. Good observations are praised, sketches that have noted some detail are held up. The children are directed to measure their leaves as exactly as possible. We get them to record overall length and width, and depending upon the leaf shape we may measure from the stem base to point extremities. We may calculate the ratios between measurements if the pupils are able to do this computation. All the measurement will create another set of data to record on the chalkboard as the class brainstorms. The teacher puts a leaf on the overhead projector to enlarge the edges, commenting with the children about the texture and composition. Each pupil gets a turn to place his or her own leaf on the lighted surface to study the veining and the cellular composition. Their observations are incorporated into their sketches.

Finally the class brainstorms as the teacher records the leaf characteristics on the chalkboard. Together they note the number of veins, major and minor, checking to see if all the leaves are the same. They count the number of points or projections in each leaf. They tabulate their measurements to create a table which they later use to write a paragraph. They record the colors, the feel, the shape, getting into metaphor with phrases such as "it feels like _____," "it looks like _____," or "the leaf is the color of _____." They contrast the two surfaces. They blow on the leaf or wave it in the air to simulate the wind, listing words to describe its movement.

This mass of information becomes a bank of information to create various kinds of paragraphs. The phrases are put onto sentence strips to make classification and reclassification easy. Pupils write factually, scientifically, as accurately as possible in creating textlike prose. They use the same information to create song and poetry describing their leaves.

We have had children select some small portion of the outdoor world, a fork in a tree, a ten- or twenty-inch portion of a branch, the ground encircled by a stretched-open coat hanger, a bird's nest, etc. Sometimes we have children work in groups of two to four to make the observations. They record the location as accurately as possible so that repeated observations are possible. Together the children make observations and write descriptive paragraphs. They visit the spot weekly, making repeated observations, noting change and lack of change. Usually this develops into a recording of the seasons. Through this process children become independent in the work of observing and recording data. We can do a similar thing within the classroom by building a small terrarium containing a rotting log, which is guaranteed to yield lots of changes as bug and plant life appear. With all of this we do lots of sketching, and sometimes we get into the business of photographing to augment our sketches and print observations.

10

For Parents and Nonteachers

Parents are sometimes afraid or awed at the thought that they might be expected to do things to teach their child to read. They worry that the schools are not doing the job, but they also worry that they may interfere with the school's methods. Some are even concerned that they might inadvertently teach, fearing that this will conflict with the teaching at school. Learning to read may be exceedingly complex, but this is no reason for alarm. The learning may be complex, but the teaching need not be. Learning to read should be no more complex than learning to speak. Parents are the main teachers of speech; they merely do what comes naturally, and speech emerges. Teaching a child to read should be equally straightforward and fairly simple.

Part of the confusion comes from defining what reading is. The best definition we know came from a seven-year-old who said, when asked what reading was, "Reading is getting the thoughts of others about things." We agree. Reading has to do with the getting of meanings and messages, and with the getting of the thoughts of authors. Note, the child said nothing about the words or the saying of words. Similarly, no one ever thinks of listening as the hearing of words. When listening we do not think of the individual words and pronounce them to ourselves in order to get the meaning. It is, in fact, the meaning that causes us to sometimes pay attention to the words, and usually only when the meaning is not clear. Listening is getting the thoughts of others from speech. Speech is phonetic, so that listening should require phonics, but we never worry about a child's phonics or word recognition when speaking to him or her. We are concerned that the child gets the message. As children learn to listen, they begin to respond, trying to say their own ideas. From listening and trying to speak, a child's speech emerges; there are almost daily refinements as the child becomes more and more articulate. The child uses long vowels, short vowels, consonant *141* blends, digraphs, diphthongs, etc., blending together sounds to say such complicated words as *supercalifragilisticexpialidocious* with less difficulty than the parents. All the "phonics" of speech is used with nary a rule nor a lesson, nor the conscious knowledge that individual letters or sounds exist. Children speak about the things that they experience and understand, and speech helps them further to understand. Words get attached to ideas, and sounds get joined into articulate words. The ideas come first, the attempts and practice come second, and correct enunciation comes last. Learning to read should progress in much the same fashion.

Frank Jennings has stated:

> What is reading? Where does it start? How can it be done well? With these questions you can make a fortune, wreck a school system or get elected to the board of education. Most people who try to think about reading at all conjure up these little black wriggles on a page and then mutter something about *meaning*. If this is all it is, very few of us would ever learn anything. For reading is older than printing or writing or even language itself. Reading begins with wonder at the world about us. It starts with the recognition of repeated events like thunder, lightning and rain. It starts with the seasons and the growth of things. It starts with an ache that vanished with food or water. It occurs when time is discovered. Reading begins with the management of signs of things. It begins when the mother, holding the child's hand, says that a day is *beautiful* or *cold* or that the wind is *soft*. Reading is *signs and portents*, the flight of birds, the changing moon, the *changeless* sun and the *fixed* stars that move through the night. Reading is the practical management of the world about us. It was this for the man at the cave's mouth. It is this for us at the desk, the bench, or control panel.
>
> The special kind of reading that you are doing now is the culmination of all the other kinds of reading. You are dealing with signs of things represented. You are dealing with ideas and concepts that have no material matter or substance and yet are *real*. But you cannot do this kind of reading if you have not become skilled in all the other kinds. Unless you know *down* from *up*, *hot* from *cold*, *now* from *then*, you could never learn to understand things that merely represent other things. You would have no language, as you now understand it, and you could not live in the open society of human beings. It is quite conceivable that a true non-reader can only survive in a mental hospital.[1]

Rachel Carson talks about this same process of learning language, which we will call reading readiness:

> One stormy autumn night when my nephew Roger was about twenty months old I wrapped him in a blanket and carried him down to the beach

---

1. Frank G. Jennings, *This Is Reading* (New York: Teachers College Pr., Columbia Univ., 1965), pp. 3–4.

in the rainy darkness. Out there, just at the edge of where-we-couldn't-see, big waves were thundering in, dimly seen white shapes that boomed and shouted and threw great handfuls of froth at us. Together we laughed for pure joy—he a baby meeting for the first time the wild tumult of Oceanus, I with the salt of half a lifetime of sea love in me. But I think we felt the same spine-tingling response to the vast, roaring ocean and the wild night around us. . . .

When Roger has visited me in Maine and we have walked in these woods I have made no conscious effort to name plants or animals nor to explain to him, but have just expressed my own pleasure in what we see, calling his attention to this or that but only as I would share discoveries with an older person. Later I have been amazed at the way names stick in his mind, for when I show color slides of my woods plants it is Roger who can identify them. "Oh, that's what Rachel likes—that's bunchberry!" Or, "That's Jumer—(juniper) but you can't eat those green berries—they are for the squirrels." I am sure no amount of drill would have implanted the names so firmly as just going through the woods in the spirit of two friends on an expedition of exciting discovery. . . .

A child's world is fresh and new and beautiful, full of wonder and excitement. It is our misfortune that for most of us that clear-eyed vision, that true instinct for what is beautiful and awe-inspiring, is dimmed and even lost before we reach adulthood. If I had influence with the good fairy who is supposed to preside over the christening of all children I should ask that her gift to each child in the world be a sense of wonder so indestructible that it would last throughout life, as an unfailing antidote against the boredom and disenchantments of later years, the sterile preoccupation with things that are artificial, the alienation from the sources of our strength.

If a child is to keep alive his inborn sense of wonder without any such gift from the fairies, he needs the companionship of at least one adult who can share it, rediscovering with him the joy, excitement and mystery of the world we live in. Parents often have a sense of inadequacy when confronted on the one hand with the eager, sensitive mind of a child and on the other with a world of complex physical nature, inhabited by a life so various and unfamiliar that it seems hopeless to reduce it to order and knowledge. In a mood of self-defeat, they exclaim, "How can I possibly teach my child about nature—why, I don't even know one bird from another!"

I sincerely believe that for the child, and for the parent seeking to guide him, it is not half so important to *know* as to *feel*. If facts are the seeds that later produce knowledge and wisdom, then the emotions and the impressions of the senses are the fertile soil in which the seeds must grow. The years of early childhood are the time to prepare the soil. Once the emotions have been aroused—a sense of the beautiful, the excitement of the new and the unknown, a feeling of sympathy, pity, admiration or love—then we wish for knowledge about the object of our emotional response. Once found, it has lasting meaning. It is more important to pave the way for the child to want to know than to put him on a diet of facts he is not ready to assimilate.[2]

Walt Whitman spoke of this same kind of reading readiness in *Leaves of Grass*.

> There was a child went forth every day, and the first object he looked upon, that object he became, and that object became part of him for the day, for a certain part of the day, or for many years or stretching cycles of years. . . . [3]

We need to examine why children might want to read if we are to understand how to teach. Children read for entertainment, but other entertainments compete so well that reading for entertainment is not enough to compel children to read. Children demand more than entertainment. They want more than the ephemerality of television. They want to grow; they want to think; they want to speculate; they want to imagine; they want to learn. They want to discover their world so that they can feel secure and feel that they are a part of humanity. They do all of these things and more by "talking" with an author.

Children respond to inner pacings that cannot be met by moving stimuli. They want to look at a flower, to reflect about the stars, to feel the wind, to empathize with others. They want time to think; they want time to shop in the world of ideas without any pressure to buy. With books children can do this. They can listen to the voices of others; they can respond in a hundred ways knowing that each author is mute and cannot censure their responses.

Clifton Fadiman comments about why he read between the ages of four and fourteen.

> During those ten years I read for reading's sake. I didn't do it to learn anything, though I found later on that I had learned a lot. I didn't read to prepare myself for a grown-up career, though I found later on that my ability to read helped me to make a living. I didn't read to get ahead of anyone else, or to improve my marks in school. I read for the same reason we all like to open Christmas gifts. Each book was a surprise package stuffed with things I had no idea ever existed.
>
> I grew bug-eyed over the miracle of language. How could a few punctuation marks plus words made out of twenty-six letters be put together so as actually to *make* (inside my head) people, animal stories, landscapes, streets, towns, and even ideas? Here I was, a rather dull boy looking at an unopened book. Then within a short time the dull boy found he was entertained, amused, saddened, delighted, mystified, scared, dreamy, puzzled, astonished, held in suspense—all depending on what

2. Rachel Carson, *A Sense of Wonder* (New York: Harper, 1956), unp.
3. Walt Whitman, *Leaves of Grass* (Garden City, N.Y.: Doubleday, 1929), p. 305.

was in those pages. And sometimes he was bored—a perfectly reasonable thing to be and a good mood in which to develop judgment, for we can learn from what we dislike as well as from what we like. . . . [4]

Through reading children have the freedom to live vicariously, to learn without penalty or time limit. They can reread and reread and reread as they think and feel and learn. They learn lots of facts, but more important, they *enjoy* as authors comment about human life, as authors attempt to preserve what is fine and good and meaningful, to enable a reader now and many years hence to improve the quality of human life. Authors attempt to preserve what they think is eternal, what is true, what is beautiful, and what is mysterious. When they succeed we have a classic.

What makes a classic is the story's continuing to shine rather than tarnish with each repetition. The story gains a patina with each reading. The reader gains an increased understanding and an increased sense of mystery. It is hard to predict if a story to be published will be accepted by children; it is impossible to predict a classic. However, children have a natural talent in selecting literature and forcing preservation. Children work at solving mysteries by demanding a favorite bedtime story for months, sometimes years, and then suddenly no longer wanting to hear the story because there is no longer anything to learn or puzzle about.

Children who have been read to and who have had rich experiences with the world about them come to print and the reading of print as naturally as they came to speech. Each child heard and listened to others speak for a long period before saying anything intelligible. And then there was a long period of practicing, where mistake and error in pronunciation and syntax were more common than correctness. In learning to read there is a long period of experiencing in which the child is making sense out of the world, and learning the "simple" things such as *up* and *down*, *in* and *out*, *run* and *ran* as well as *dog, cat, tree, rose, flower,* etc. It is during this period that mother and father read the favorite bedtime story 100 or more times, sing favorite songs and recite favorite poems many times. If the child asks a question about print, it is answered quickly, directly, and naturally with no attempt to teach or belabor. During this readiness children rehearse the loved story by saying it to themselves in whatever oral language they know. Fortunately many children do this rehearsing audibly, or we might not know that it occurs. They often "read" to a teddy bear or a dog. They say the ideas, and their rehearsals become more and more exactly like the printed text as long as

---

4. Clifton Fadiman, "Let's Talk," in *The World Treasury of Children's Literature* (Boston: Little, Brown, 1984), p. xiv.

they continue to hear the real version. They become so accurate in their memories that some children appear to be reading. We have known many children at this stage who have stated, "I love to read this book. Listen. I can read it without looking."

It is later, sometimes much later, that they begin to unravel the mysteries of print by working with well-known texts. Our own six children all were read to, sung to, and talked to from birth. They were walked with, taken in the supermarket shopping basket, and talked to on repeated trips. They became interested in print and its mysteries at ages three through nine. The late starters were taught at age six in school, and they learned to recognize enough words to satisfy the school's demands—not, however, without being suggested for special help. They are now adult and fully literate; it would be impossible for anyone to determine which child began to read at three and which at nine. The late starters were more interested in other parts of their world, so much so that they could not be bothered with print until they had learned to read lots of other signs and portents more important to them than print.

Unfortunately, today there is near hysteria about beginning reading early and particularly about the need to recognize words accurately. We have people advocating the use of flash cards with infants so that the baby must point to *milk* before being fed. We have preschools advertising that they will teach the alphabet and phonics to three-year-old children and that their preschool requires academic work. We have daily homework required by school-board mandate in kindergarten so that children will learn how to cope with the demands of grade one. Childhood should be a secure, unpressured time for social learnings of an intellectual nature. Children in a stimulating environment impose their own demands and learn without outside pressures. The brain is born to learn language and cannot refuse to learn unless is has been corrupted. Children do not need demands and pressure. They need opportunity. Unfortunately, childhood has become a time for testing, for meeting overt (usually meaningless) performance criteria, for running a race. Childhood as a time for practicing, for rehearsing language with all the accompanying mistakes that are a natural part of rehearsing, has vanished, to be replaced by step-by-step "learning" with perfect performance. We have become obsessed with superficial symptoms and forgotten what is requisite for literacy. In our race to achieve skills in reading we have created achievement-test scores that are no more reflective of reading than theater sets are of the buildings and trees that we "see" on stage. We have lost faith in the power of language, in children's books, and in other literature, and we no longer believe in the innate power to learn language born into every child's brain. We seem not to care if a child does read, can read, or wants to read. We seem only to care about good scores on the reading tests given many times during the year.

We knew of one child of seven who read anything and everything. One of her favorite activities was to write short stories and poetry. She expressed herself clearly and sensitively, with rarely a mistake in spelling. She failed phonics on her grade-two report card in four marking periods. This was a child who understood phonics. She used it to write and to read without having been taught formally the rules and regulations. She didn't know the terminology about long and short vowels, about syllables or the silent *e* or the format of the worksheets and tests. The school, of course, did care about "basics." The teacher first suggested remedial reading, and, in June, repeating grade two. The parents changed schools. Most parents, however, do no have this option or the understanding to choose it. We have witnessed similar concerns from teachers as they taught our own children. These were well meaning, dedicated teachers oppressed by accountability programs imposed from on high.

We can think of only one analogy to illustrate this hysteria. A farmer planted some wheat and went to the bank for a loan. The banker demanded to see the wheat to determine if it were sterile or germinating. The farmer asked the banker to wait, but he also asked for his money, to no avail, so he dug up several handfuls of wheat and took it to the banker. The banker demanded to see all the wheat. The farmer dug up all the seed, got his loan, and replanted the wheat. The little seed that grew was deformed. The banker was pleased to see that his suspicion had been confirmed.

Language learning is a social activity, whether the form be print or speech. Twins demonstrate this by inventing their own languages even when they are in a fully languaging environment, and particularly if they are not. Speaking is learned through interchange where ideas and feelings are transmitted, responded to and reacted to. Reading is learned through being read to and by the social interchange as the reader and child respond together to the ideas found in the text. There is the warm sharing of ideas and emotions, just as there is when two people share a sunrise or the beauty of a flower. Sometimes there is very little overt language, but there is a mutual interchange. There is no competition to see who can see the sunrise best or first, but each viewer seeks to share the beauty, the awe, the wonder of the sight with whomever is near. The more sharing, the richer the experience.

Reading to children should be the same kind of sharing experience. It should be done because the reader and the listener are mutual viewers of a "sunrise" which they share, and as with each morning there is a new sunrise, so with each rereading of a loved book there are new sunrises.

These experiences result in an implanting of the melodies of print within the brain of the child, but the purpose in reading to a child is to share the child's joy and clear, fresh perceptions of the book.

Children respond to language according to their ability to apprehend the ideas expressed. Apprehension is what the brain does intuitively in learning language, and the brain apprehends by using what it already has stored within itself. A young child says "cow" in response to seeing any four-legged animal except dogs and cats, which are already known, until becoming ready to see something peculiarly different that separates cows from horses, pigs, goats, zebras, and even elephants. We don't know what that difference is, nor do we know what happens in the brain as it notes *cowness* from *horseness* from *pigness*. We just know that it learns to do this from repeated experiences with cows more than repeated experiences with all noncows. When the brain is ready to see a cow, the child no longer says *cow* when a horse appears, even though the child does not yet know *horse*. Learning (concept development) comes from experiences repeated, with each repeated experience different because previous experiences affect apprehension. Each sunrise is different, and yet each is the same. If they were not the same, we could not have developed the concept *sunrise*.

Language learning comes from socially sharing experiences. Through language we communicate what is common, and that commonness permits the language to be learned. This is a wordy way of saying that parents should share experiences with children and talk to them about their experiences. The experiences should be repeated experiences more than startling, different, new experiences. Every parent knows the distress of having taken a too young child on a special trip to see Mount Rushmore, or the Empire State Building, only to discover that the child's memory of the trip is of the large hot dogs or the special bag of popcorn. Children cannot bring enough apprehension to strange new things to comprehend much in one encounter. A "Rachel Carson walk" around the yard outside the house, or a walk to the corner store in the city noting all the things that you see each time, commenting about their brilliance, their beauty, or even their shabbiness, is more valuable than special trips.

To summarize, adults who are not in the paid role of teacher should do the following things if they want the children around them to become literate:

1. Read orally to them, repeating favorite stories many times.
2. Use poetry and chants as a natural activity to pass "blah" times when driving, getting up, or going to bed.
3. Walk and talk with children, particularly a repeated walk such as going to the store.

4. As adults, read and write for adult reasons when children are able to observe. Don Holdaway has noted in *Foundations of Literacy* that young children in any culture learn any adult skill that the children observe the adult doing so long as the reason is not to get the child to learn. This is why school demonstrations by teachers sometimes do not result in children's trying to learn.[5]
5. Buy children books as presents. Ownership of at least some books is very important to children.
6. Visit children's libraries and borrow books together.

Some of our favorite authors are noted in the bibliography that follows this chapter. We must warn the reader that even the two authors of this book do not agree in liking all the same books or poems. Liking is a very personal affair, and you must read books to children that please you, not them, and repeat those which please you both. Children need to know that there are some books you do not enjoy, so that they learn that it is all right to admit that they do not like all books. Further we hesitate to list authors because there are so many fine authors that we do not know who are certainly as good as those we do know. We just haven't read their books. Having said all that, we list our favorite authors and some of their books.

One Last Note

Phonics is perhaps the one issue about which parents and teachers worry the most. We have concerned ourselves with phonics in the other chapters of this book, particularly in chapter 5; we may repeat ourselves a bit in this final comment. There are over 200 phonics programs published and sold in the United States, and probably as many more sold outside the United States. Each program has its advocates and demonstrated success based upon reading-test scores of children who use the program. The issue, to us, is not early achievement on test scores or in pronouncing words. Our concern is that we know of no evidence that suggests that early phonics, early achievement on standardized tests, or early attention to saying words leads to later higher achievement in reading, spelling, or writing. By early we mean age six and younger. We also know that many children become terribly confused when taught phonics early. They fail to understand the purpose of reading—communication with an author—because the purpose of all phonics programs is to pronounce words correctly. This misunderstanding is

5. Don Holdaway, *Foundations of Literacy* (Sidney: Ashton-Scholastic, 1978).

particularly evident in children who bear the heinous labels *dyslexic, learning disabled, mentally retarded, English as a second language,* and *disadvantaged.*

We do not define phonics as knowing that *ou* is a vowel digraph, that *ough* is a quadragraph. It is knowing that *d o g* is dog because in the sentence *The _____ barked,* the word *dog* makes sense and because the reader "thinks" that *dog* should be spelled with a *d* at the beginning, a *g* at the end, and it should have a vowel letter in the middle. Phonics is knowing that the word *dough* in the sentence *The baker mixed the dough,* must be *d o u g h* because, "If I needed to write *dough* but didn't know how to spell it, I would write *d o* and some other letter or letters because I know *d o* spells *do.*"

We do not define phonics as knowing that *e* on the end of a word is silent and the vowel up front is long, a commonly taught rule. For a child, phonics is knowing that *see same* is really *sesame,* as in sesame seed buns "which I get at Cafe Marie at our corner where I have been walking with my father for many years. Cafe Marie was one of the first signs I could read." (In this paragraph note that the words *rule, cafe, where, have,* and *one* are supposed to fit the rule. There are no words in the paragraph that do. In the preceding paragraph *because, makes, sense, have, middle, sentence,* and *write* end in *e* and should fit the rule. Only *make* and *write* do. A rule that works only two in twelve times is hardly worth trying to use. This sample is a bit harsh; research shows that the rule works about 40 percent of the time if a word is counted only once. It works less for running words because the most commonly used words are considered exceptions [*have, done, gone, come, there, where, one, are*].)

Our concern is that hours are used each week to teach some reading-phonics skills that could be learned at six or seven in a matter of minutes. Our concern is that the time left in schools for reading to children, for them to explore their world, for teachers to *prepare the soil,* to use Rachel Carson's term, is not available. Our concern is one of priorities and sensibility. Florence Goodenough demonstrated in 1928 that mentally retarded children of age three could be taught the alphabet and to say words. Obviously learning the alphabet and "reading words" does not demand high intelligence, and we wish that parents and teachers of three-, four-, five- and six-year-old children would concern themselves with concept development and understandings, with putting in the sounds of literature by reading to children, with sharing daily the marvels of the everyday world—sunlight, rain, flowers, and trees, or automobiles, television, sidewalks, and escalators. A child can apprehend, therefore read, only with what is already stored within his or her brain. We need to be much more concerned with the ideas and the quality of language stored within the brain than we do with the nuts and bolts of the alphabet as words and ideas are represented. The nuts and bolts of reading can be taught easily and efficiently in grades one and two if the child's brain is already filled with ideas and the sounds of printed language.

Bibliography

Allard, Harry. *Miss Nelson Has a Field Day*. Boston: Houghton Mifflin, 1985.
Allen, Pamela. *Bertie and the Bear*. New York: Coward-McCann, 1983.
———. *Who Sank the Boat?* New York: Coward-McCann, 1982.
Anno, Mitsumasa. *Anno's Counting House*. New York: Philomel, 1982.
Babbitt, Natalie. *The Something*. New York: Farrar, Straus, 1970.
———. *Tuck Everlasting*. New York: Farrar, Straus, 1975.
Barton, Byron. *Building a House*. New York: Greenwillow, 1981.
Behn, Harry. *All Kinds of Time*. New York: Harcourt, 1950.
Beyond the High Hills, a Book of Eskimo Poems. Photographs by Guy Mary-Rousseliere. Cleveland: Collins/World, 1961.
Bishop, Claire Huchet, and Kurt Wiese. *The Five Chinese Brothers*. New York: Coward-McCann, 1938.
Bodeker, N. M. *Hurry, Hurry Mary Dear*. New York: Atheneum, 1976.
Brittain, Bill. *Devil's Donkey*. New York: Harper & Row, 1981.
Brown, Margaret Wise. *Nibble, Nibble*. New York: Young Scott Books, 1959.
———. *The Noisy Book* and *The Seashore Noisy Book*. New York: Harper & Row, 1939.
———. *Wheel on the Chimney*. Philadelphia: Lippincott, 1954.
Bruna, Dick. *I Can Read*. London: Metheun Children's Books, 1968.
———. *My Shirt Is White*. New York: Metheun, 1972.
Bryan, Ashley. *The Dancing Granny*. New York: Atheneum, 1977.
Bulla, Clyde Robert. *Shoe Shine Girl*. New York: Crowell, 1975.
———. *The Sword in the Tree*. New York: Crowell, 1956.
———, and Michael Syson. *Conquista!* New York: Crowell, 1978.
Burningham, John. *The Dog*. New York: Crowell, 1975.
———. *The Shopping Basket*. New York: Crowell, 1980.
———. *Would You Rather?* New York: Crowell, 1978.
Carrick, Carol. *The Accident*. New York: Clarion, 1976.
Cole, William. *Frances Face-Maker*. Cleveland: Collins/World, 1963.
Dahl, Roald. *Fantastic Mr. Fox*. New York: Knopf, 1970.
De Paola, Tomie. *The Cloud Book*. New York: Scholastic, 1975.

————. *Fin M'Coul, the Giant of Knockmany Hill.* New York: Holiday House, 1981.

————. *The Friendly Beasts, an Old English Christmas Carol.* New York: Putnam's, 1981.

————. *Maryanna May and Nursey.* New York: Holiday House, 1983.

————. *Nanny Upstairs and Nanny Downstairs.* New York: Putnam's, 1973.

————. *Now One Foot, Now the Other.* New York: Putnam's, 1981.

————. *The Quicksand Book.* New York: Holiday House, 1977.

————. *Strega Nona.* Englewood Cliffs, N.J.: Prentice-Hall, 1975.

De Regniers, Beatrice Schenk. *Going for a Walk.* New York: Harper & Row, 1961.

————. *What Can You Do with a Shoe?* New York: Harper, 1955.

Degen, Bruce. *Jamberry.* New York: Harper & Row, 1983.

Dodd, Lynley. *Hairy Maclary, from Donaldson's Dairy.* Wellington, New Zealand: Mallinson Rendel, 1983.

Fadiman, Clifton. *The World Treasury of Children's Literature.* Vols. 1 & 2. Boston: Little, Brown, 1984.

Fisher, Aileen. *Out in the Dark and Daylight.* New York: Harper & Row, 1980.

Fowke, Edith. *Ring around the Moon.* Toronto: McClelland & Stewart, 1977.

Fox Went Out on a Chilly Night, an Old Song. Illus. by Peter Spier. Garden City, N.Y.: Doubleday, 1961.

Gag, Wanda. *Tales from Grimm.* Vols. 1 & 2. New York: Coward-McCann, 1936.

Galdone, Johanna. *The Little Girl and the Big Bear.* Illus. by Paul Galdone. New York: Houghton Mifflin/Clarion, 1980.

Galdone, Paul. *The Elves and the Shoemaker.* New York: Clarion, 1984.

————. *The Little Red Hen.* New York: Seabury, 1973.

————. *The Magic Porridge Pot.* New York: Clarion, 1976.

Gannett, Ruth Stiles. *My Father's Dragon.* New York: Random House, 1948.

Ginsburg, Mirra. *The Chick and the Duckling.* New York: Macmillan, 1972.

————. *The Sun's Asleep behind the Hill.* New York: Greenwillow, 1982.

Goble, Paul. *The Girl Who Loved Wild Horses.* Scarsdale, N.Y.: Bradbury, 1978.

Grahame, Kenneth. *The Reluctant Dragon.* New York: Holiday House, 1938.

Hall, Donald. *Oxcart Man.* New York: Viking, 1979.

Harper, Wilhelmina. *The Gunniwolf.* New York: Dutton, 1967.

Heide, Florence Parry, and Roxanne Heide. *A Monster Is Coming! A Monster Is Coming!* New York: Franklin Watts, 1980.

Heller, Ruth. *Animals Born Alive and Well.* New York: Grosset & Dunlap, 1982.

————. *Chickens Aren't the Only Ones.* New York: Grosset & Dunlap, 1982.

Herriot, James. *Moses the Kitten.* London: Michael Joseph/Adam & Charles Black, 1974.

————. *Only One Woof.* New York: St. Martin's, 1974, 1985.

Hill, Eric. *Where's Spot?* New York: Putnam, 1981. (There are five other books in the series as well.)

Himler, Ronald. *Wake Up, Jeremiah.* New York: Harper & Row, 1979.

Hoban, Russell. *Bread and Jam for Frances.* New York: Harper & Row, 1964.

Hoberman, Mary Anne. *A House Is a House for Me.* New York: Viking, 1978.

Hutchins, Pat. *Don't Forget the Bacon.* New York: Greenwillow, 1976.

————. *Follow That Bus*. New York: Greenwillow, 1967.

————. *King Henry's Palace*. New York: Greenwillow, 1983.

————. *One Hunter*. New York: Greenwillow, 1982.

————. *Rosie's Walk*. New York: Macmillan, 1968.

————. *The Very Worst Monster*. New York: Greenwillow, 1985.

Jarrell, Randall. *The Bat Poet*. New York: Macmillan, 1963.

Jewell, Nancy. *Time for Uncle Joe*. New York: Harper & Row, 1981.

Kalan, Robert. *Blue Sea*. New York: Greenwillow, 1979.

Keats, Ezra Jack. *Apartment Three*. New York: Macmillan, 1971.

King, Deborah. *Puffin*. New York: Lothrop, 1984.

Krauss, Ruth. *The Happy Egg*. New York: Scholastic, 1967.

————. *The Little King, The Little Queen, The Little Monster and Other Stories You Can Make Up Yourself*. New York: Scholastic, 1964.

————, and Crockett Johnson. *Is This You?* New York: Scholastic, 1955.

Kuskin, Karla. *Dogs and Dragons, Trees and Dreams*. New York: Harper & Row, 1980.

————. *Sand and Snow*. New York: Harper & Row, 1965.

Lane, Margaret. *The Beaver*. New York: Dial, 1982.

————. *The Fish*. New York: Dial, 1982.

————. *The Fox*. New York: Dial, 1982.

————. *The Frog*. New York: Dial, 1982.

————. *The Spider*. New York: Dial, 1982.

————. *The Squirrel*. New York: Dial, 1982.

Leaf, Munro. *Wee Gillis*. New York: Viking, 1938.

Lee, Dennis. *Lizzi's Lion*. Toronto: Stoddart, 1984.

————. *The Ordinary Bath*. Toronto: Magcook, 1979.

Lester, Helen. *It Wasn't My Fault*. Boston: Houghton Mifflin, 1985.

Lionni, Leo. *Frederick*. New York: Knopf/Pantheon, 1967.

Lund, Doris Herold. *The Paint-Box Sea*. New York: McGraw-Hill, 1973.

Kimmel, Margaret Mary. *Magic in the Mist*. New York: Atheneum, 1976.

McCloskey, Robert. *Make Way for Ducklings*. New York: Viking, 1941.

McCord, David. *One at a Time*. Boston: Little, Brown, 1974.

————. *Speak Up*. Boston: Little, Brown, 1979, 1980.

McDonald, Golden (Margaret Wise Brown). *A Little Island*. Garden City, N.Y.: Doubleday, 1946.

Miles, Miska. *Annie and the Old One*. Boston: Little, Brown, 1971.

Milne, A. A. *Now We Are Six*. New York: Dutton, 1927.

————. *When We Were Very Young*. New York: Dutton, 1924.

————. *Winnie the Pooh*. New York: Dutton, 1926.

Moore, Lilian. *I Thought I Heard the City*. New York: Atheneum, 1969.

Mowat, Farley. *Owl in the Family*. Boston: Little, Brown, 1961.

Myers, Walter D. *The Dragon Takes His Wife*. Indianapolis: Bobbs-Merrill, 1972.

Norton, Mary. *Bed-Knobs and Broom Sticks*. New York: Harcourt, 1957.

Olsen, Ib Spang. *The Marsh Crone's Brew*. New York and Nashville: Abington, 1960.

Paterson, A. B. *Waltzing Matilda*. Sidney, Australia: William Collins, 1970.

A Peaceable Kingdom, a Shaker Abecedarius. Illus. by Alice and Martin Provensen. New York: Viking, 1978.

Prelutsky, Jack. *It's Halloween*. New York: Greenwillow, 1977.

————. *The New Kid on the Block*. New York: Greenwillow, 1984.

————. *The Queen of Eene*. New York: Greenwillow, 1970, 1978.

————. *The Snopp on the Sidewalk and Other Poems*. New York: Greenwillow, 1976, 1977.

————, ed. *The Random House Book of Poetry for Children*. New York: Random House, 1983.

Raffi. *Baby Baluga Book*. Toronto: McClelland & Stewart, 1983.

Rawls, Wilson. *Where the Red Fern Grows*. New York: Doubleday, 1961.

Richler, Mordecai. *Jacob Two-Two Meets the Hooded Fang*. New York: Knopf, 1975.

Rockwell, Anne. *First Comes Spring*. New York: Crowell, 1985.

————. *The Old Woman and Her Pig and Ten Other Stories*. New York: Crowell, 1979.

Roughsey, Dick. *The Rainbow Serpent*. Sydney, Australia: William Collins, 1975.

Ryder, Joanne. *Fog in the Meadow*. New York: Harper & Row, 1979.

————. *The Spider's Dance*. New York: Harper & Row, 1981.

Sandburg, Carl. *Rootabaga Stories*. New York: Harcourt, 1922, 1923.

Schecter, Ben. *Sparrow Song*. New York: Harper & Row, 1981.

Scheer, Julian, and Marvin Bileck. *Rain Makes Applesauce*. New York: Holiday House, 1964.

Sendak, Maurice. *Seven Little Monsters*. New York: Harper & Row, 1975.

————. *The Nutshell Library*. New York: Harper & Row, 1962.

Serraillier, Ian. *Suppose You Met a Witch*. Boston: Little, Brown, 1973.

Shannon, George. *Bean Boy*. New York: Greenwillow, 1984.

————. *Dance Away*. New York: Greenwillow, 1982.

————. *Lizard Song*. New York: Greenwillow, 1981.

————. *The Piney Woods Peddler*. New York: Greenwillow, 1981.

Sharon, Lois, and Bram. *Elephant Jam*. Toronto: McGraw-Hill Ryerson, 1980.

Shulevitz, Uri. *Rain, Rain, Rivers*. New York: Farrar, Straus, 1969.

Simon, Mina Lewiton. *Is Anyone Here?* New York: Atheneum, 1967.

Singer, Isaac Bashevis. *Zlatah the Goat and Other Stories*. New York: Harper & Row, 1966.

Singing Bee! Collection of Favorite Children's Songs. Comp. by Jane Hart. New York: Lothrop, 1982.

Slobodkina, Esphyr. *Caps for Sale*. New York: Scholastic, 1940.

Smith, Gene. *The Visitor*. New York: Cowles, 1971.

Stren, Patti. *There's a Rainbow in My Closet*. New York: Harper & Row, 1979.

Sutton, Eve. *My Cat Likes to Hide in Boxes*. New York: Puffin/Penguin, 1973, 1978.

Tashjian, Virginia A. *Juba This and Juba That*. Boston: Little, Brown, 1969.

Tresselt, Alvin. *What Did You Leave Behind?* New York: Lothrop, 1978.

Tripp, Wallace. *Granfa Grig Had a Pig*. Boston: Little, Brown, 1976.

————. *A Great Big Ugly Man Came Up and Tied His Horse to Me, a Book of Nonsense Verse*. Boston: Little, Brown, 1973.

Ungerer, Tomi. *The Three Robbers*. New York: Atheneum, 1962.

Wallace, Daisy, ed. *Witch Poems*. New York: Holiday House, 1976.

Wells, Rosemary. *Martha's Birthday*. Englewood Cliffs, N.J.: Bradbury, 1970.

White, E. B. *Charlotte's Web*. New York: Harper & Row, 1952.

Zemach, Harvey. *The Judge*. New York: Farrar, Straus, 1969.

Zolotow, Charlotte. *I Know a Lady*. New York: Greenwillow, 1984.

———. *If You Listen*. New York: Harper & Row, 1980.

Robert A. McCracken and Marlene J. McCracken share an international reputation as experts in primary education. Robert A. McCracken is currently professor of education at Western Washington University in Bellingham; he has also served as a reading consultant and reading teacher. Marlene J. McCracken is a consultant in primary education with more than 35 years experience in teaching primary reading. She is currently district language teacher for the Surrey, B.C., School District. The McCrackens have collaborated on several books, including *Reading, Writing, and Language* (Winnipeg: Peguis Press, 1979) and have presented workshops and seminars in the United States, Canada, England, Germany, Australia, and Hong Kong.